CONTRIBUTIONS BY

ALEC LUU

ARON MILLER

JEAN HSI

JON KIM

JOSE MONTANO

THOMAS MILLER

ALEC

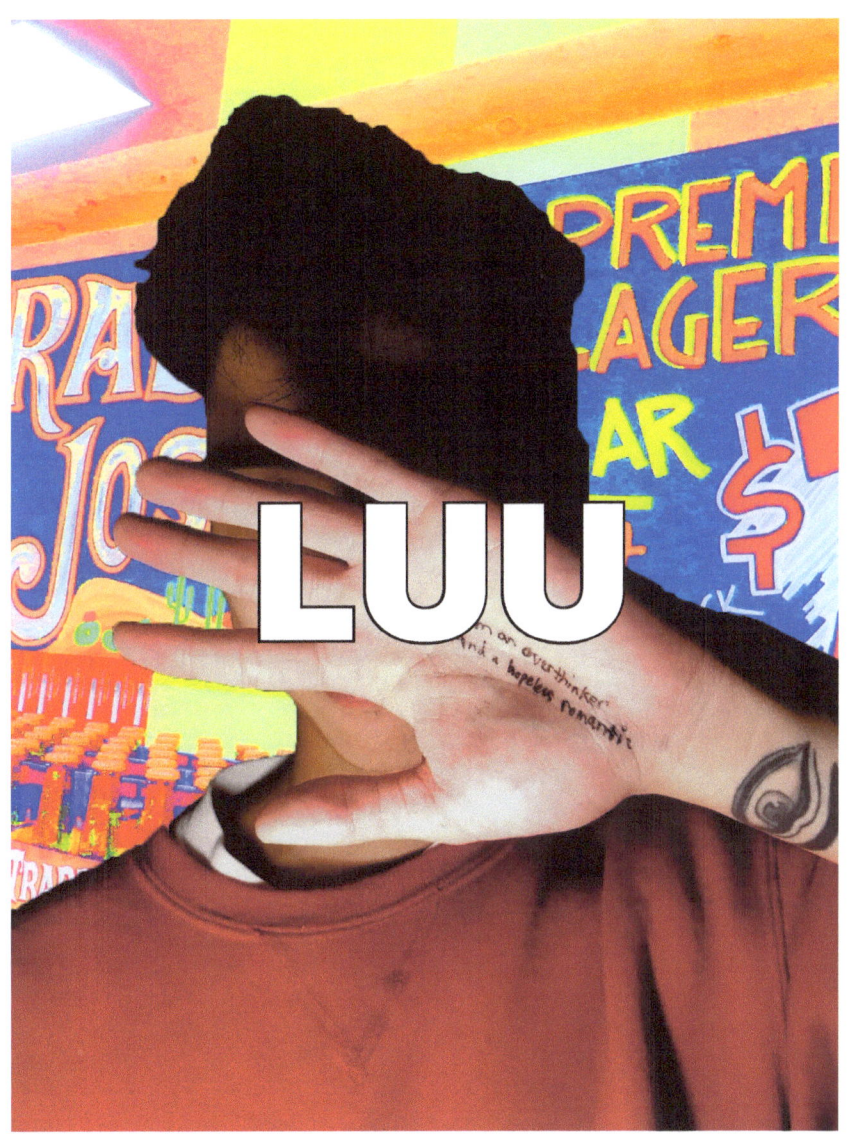

i am an overthinker and a hopeless romantic

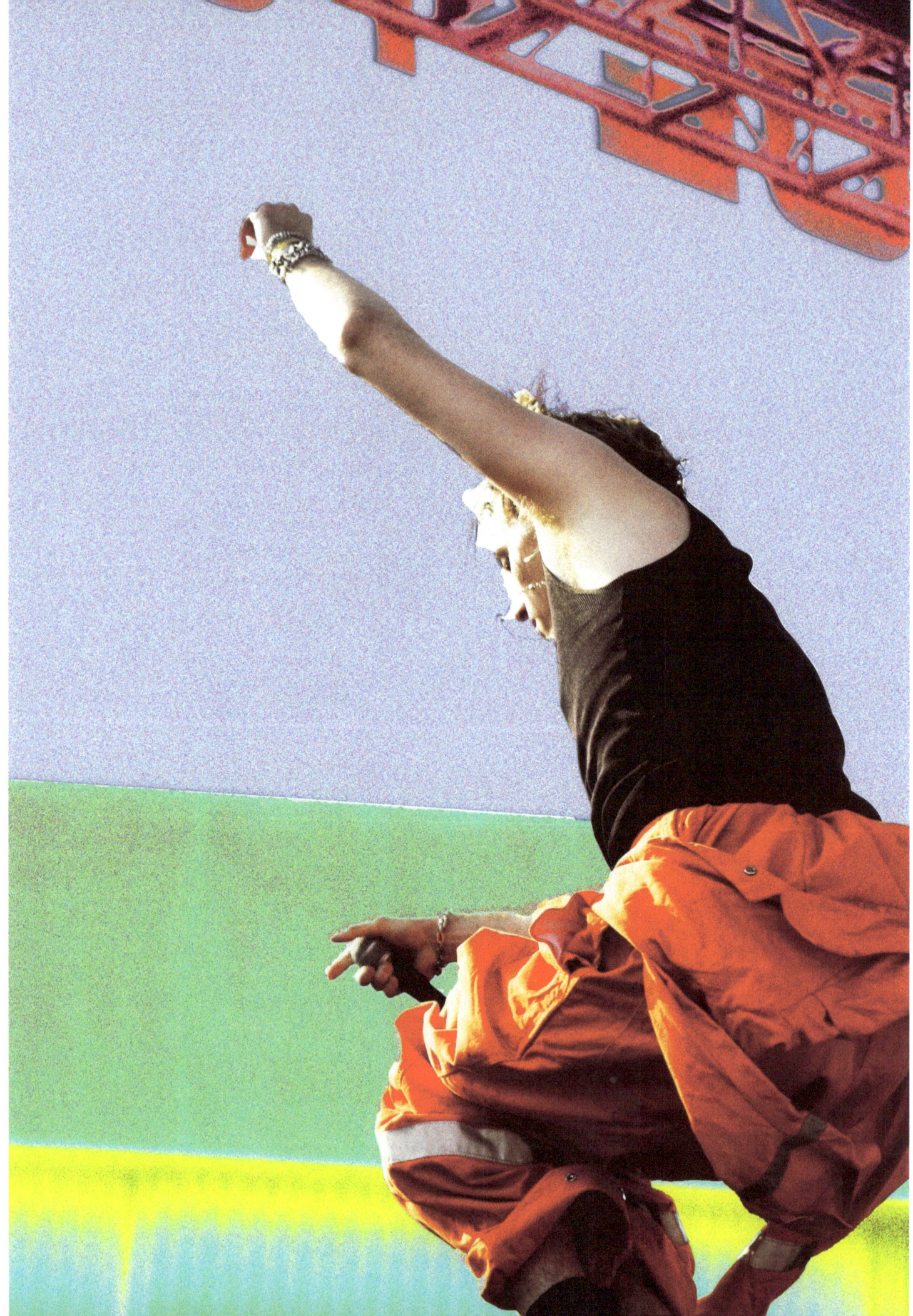

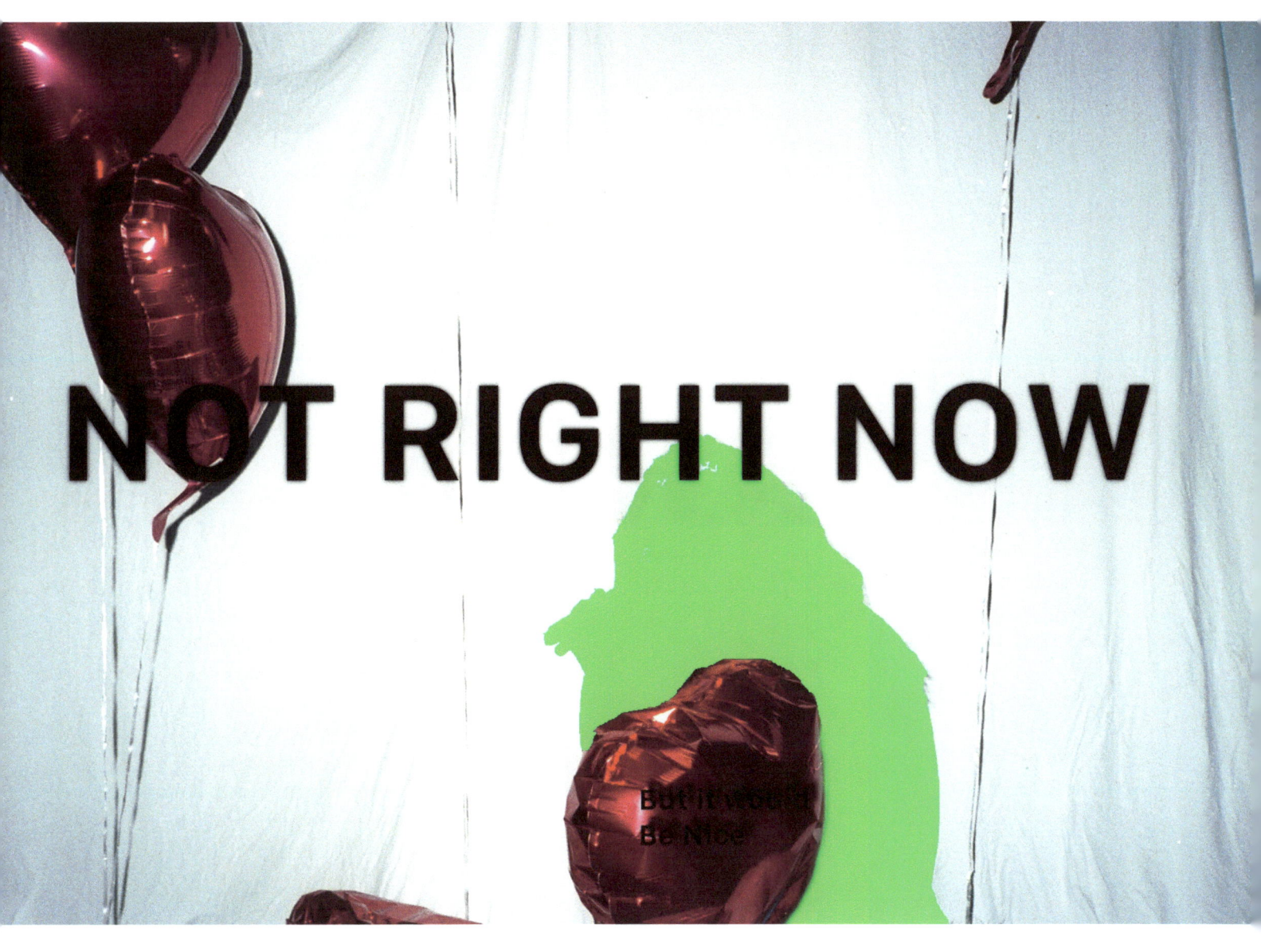

ARON

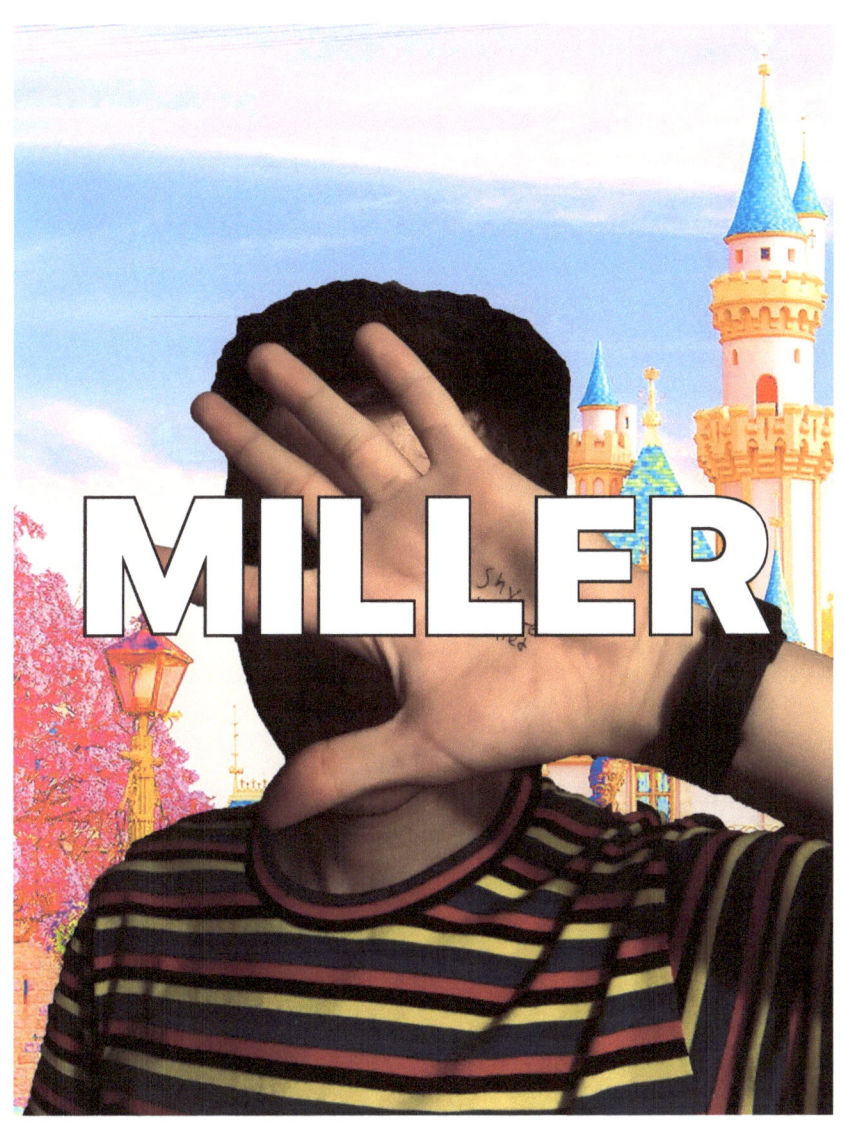

shy insecure quiet

Froth

A short story by Aron Miller

Max smiled ironically at the waiter (Arthur) as he (the waiter) passed by and—finally—didn't ask if they needed anything. Joan, across the table from Max, slowly sipped on her frothy pink lemonade shake and smiled at him with her eyes. He was half stiff and only getting stiffer. Big, green eyes.

How's your shake? He liked to see her face in motion.

She took a big, long sip from the curly straw. It's pretty good. Are you sure you don't want any?

No thanks. It looks too much like strawberry. It did.

You don't like strawberry? She was only slightly surprised.

Well, I don't mind strawberry, but it's sort of like—my taste buds would get all fucked up expecting strawberry and then getting lemon. Hahaha.

I don't think it would be that bad. She just wanted him to try it. She also didn't want to talk about the shake.

I just don't really want any. He did, but he didn't.

Max had a root beer float in front of him. He had only taken a sip of it when the waiter had first brought it out. He didn't even really like root beer; he just got it to have something to drink with Joan. It was quickly approaching room temperature at this point. The float had cost five dollars, so that kind of sucked.

Joan looked down at her shake and took another sip.

Arthur watched the couple from behind the counter. He was jealous. How had these two met? School? Work? Mutual friends? He, too, had tried those outlets. None of them had worked, and he was getting more anxious as each year passed. Plenty of fish in the sea, they say. But it seemed like his worm just wasn't good enough bait.

In any case, this girl was pretty good lookin'. She had on a striped crop top and high-waisted jeans that showed just enough of her smooth, toned navel area to hint at how good the the rest of her body looked. It gave him a hard-on. Fuck, why doesn't porn use outfits like this?

Her dyed red hair was in a messy ponytail that looked really good and brought out the shape of her face nicely.

The guy she was with seemed to fit her though. One of those skater boys—rolled pant cuffs, unbuttoned button-up shirt, ragged old vans. The guy had given him a funny look earlier and it made Arthur afraid to go and ask if they needed any refills or extra napkins. So he just sat behind the front counter and checked her out. His boner was becoming more and more solid. He looked down and could see a clear lump growing in his pants' crotch.

A small group walked in—Rick, Gen, Monique, Alex, and Diego—for a post-movie snack. Rick went up to the counter to check in for a table. The waiter had a bit of a stressed out look on his face, like he wasn't capable of doing his job right at the moment.

You can take a seat anywhere. The waiter shuffled some papers around on the counter and waited for the group of kids to pick a table.

Ok, cool. Rick looked at his friends and pointed to a booth by a window overlooking the street. They all went and took their seats.

Gen slid into the seat on the right side of the table (assuming you're looking out through the window, looking at the street) and Monique slid in after her. Diego stood, assessing the situation, waiting for the others to take their seats. Rick and Alex slid in opposite of Gen and Monique, respectively. Diego went to sit next to Monique, keeping the table from suffering an unacknowledged, but still very real, tension from a gender divide. Before he sat, however, Gen said thus:

Oh wait, I need to use the restroom.

So Diego, who had a cheek already contacting the edge of his seat, had to stop himself mid-motion and stand back up. Monique, who had put her purse down after she slid into her spot, picked up her purse and slid back out and stood to let Gen out. Gen put her phone on the table, as if to leave it there as she used the baño, and started to slide out, but then changed her mind about leaving her phone, stopped, grabbed her phone again, finally slid all the way out, and hurried over to the corner of the diner where the restroom was.

Diego looked at Monique, waiting for her to get back in.

Monique noticed.

I'll just wait for her to come back.

Diego didn't particularly feel like standing anymore, so he sat where he had planned to sit before Gen decided she needed to get up. They waited for about 30 seconds, and then Monique took the empty spot next to Alex. Another 30 seconds and Rick, who had been looking out the window this entire time, turned to his friends and made a pertinent observation.

Where's our menus?

Hmm.

Just then, Gen returned from the bathroom. Diego got up and let her in. She got back in, and slid down to her spot across from Rick. Diego looked at Monique, who gave a sarcastic smile and got up and then got back into her original spot next to Gen and across from Alex. Diego finally planted himself in his seat.

Alex looked at the counter where the lone waiter was still sitting. The waiter was staring at the space in front of him, as if he was bored or in deep focus.

He's just sitting there.

Go ask him for our menus.

Alex slid out of the booth seat and went over to the counter where the waiter was sitting. The waiter coldly watched him as he approached.

Um, excuse me, can we get some menus?

Oh, yeah, sorry about that. I'll bring them right to your table.

The high school kid turned and walked back to his table where his friends were still waiting quietly. Arthur looked down. The time had come; he had to take care of business. The boner he had developed over the previous few minutes still had not subsided. In fact, it was in all likelihood only getting more solid. He would have to take a quick bathroom break to get this sorted out once he finished with these kids. But first, he had to make sure the bump in his pants wasn't going to be visible when he took the menus over.

Fortunately for him, his crotch region was protected from onlookers by the counter he was sitting behind, but he still made a quick scan of the room to make sure no one was watching. Then, in many disjointed and quick motions, he stuck his hands into his pockets, gripped the shaft of his penis using his pockets like gloves, shifted it from where it was caught in his underwear (and had been, as they say, "pitching a tent"), and flipped it upward so that it was braced against his lower abdomen by his underwear's waistband. He grabbed four menus and hurried them over to the kids at the table, trying to ignore all the stimulation of his dick rubbing against the elastic of his waistband.

Diego looked over and saw the waiter finally coming with their menus. He looked like he was walking kind of funny, even hunching over a little.

Here are your menus. Sorry for the wait.

It's ok!

What can I get you guys to drink?

I'll take a water.

Water for me too.

Water. He smirked.

Water for us, too.

Alright, I'll bring those right out.

There was just no way Arthur was going to be able to bring them out right away, though. This boner was becoming more and more of an issue. To make matters worse, as he turned from the table of high schoolers, he caught a nice up close glimpse of the redhead girl. She was leaned back and had an upset look on her face. Her midriff was pretty well exposed to him from the angle he was at, and the smoothness of her skin was absolutely overwhelming—his dick was throbbing at this point.

He hurried to the kitchen, where the two late night cooks were busy tidying up some equipment.

I'm going to take a quick bathroom break, can one of you watch the front for a minute?

He rushed to the bathroom before they could answer, locked the door, and unzipped.

So then why did you even ask what I thought about it?

Because I like to know what you're thinking, Joan.

You want to know what I think about this shake? It's just a shake!

Ok, you need to relax. I mean, it doesn't matter what it is, I just wanted to make conversation. Her eyes looked so different when they were squinting in frustration.

Why about this stupid shake? You could have asked me so many better things—how is a good conversation going to happen about a fucking milkshake?

Well, I don't know, I wasn't thinking that hard about it! His boner had disappeared long ago.

You're just not thinking, Max. You could have asked me about so many different things. What's my favorite movie? What are my thoughts on the military industrial complex? Have I ever thought about going vegan? At least try to get to know me!

Alright, ok. Fine. Just calm down.

Hey, we never got our waters, huh.

Nope... I don't even see the waiter anywhere.

I saw him go into the restroom. He's probably sick, that's why he's was just sitting there for so long before he gave us the menus.

Yea, probably. He didn't even bring out enough for everyone.

It's no big deal, I'm sure he'll be out in a minute.

Arthur cleaned himself up, zipped up his pants, washed his hands, and went back outside feeling much lighter. He headed to the kitchen to get the waters for the kids.

Thanks guys.

Huh?

Thanks for watching the front.

Oh man, we didn't even hear you before.

Aw jeez. Well, ok. I'm sure everything's alright anyway. It's pretty slow tonight.

He put all the waters on a tray and headed out. As he walked to the high school table, he noticed that the girl and the guy had left. He passed the waters out to the kids and then checked the table that the couple had been sitting.

Arthur hadn't given them their check yet. The shake was pretty much empty, but the root beer float was basically untouched. In the middle of the table was a single five dollar bill—about three dollars and thirty cents short of the actual cost for the two desserts.

JEAN

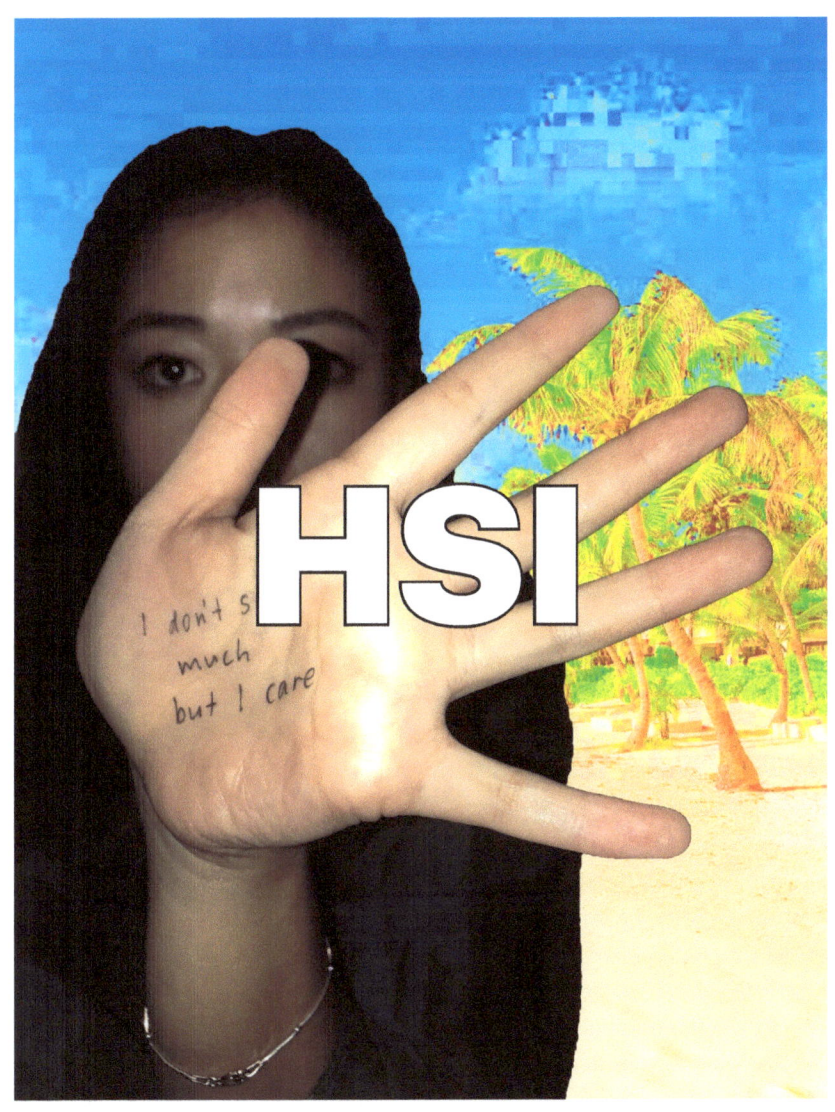

i don't say much but i care

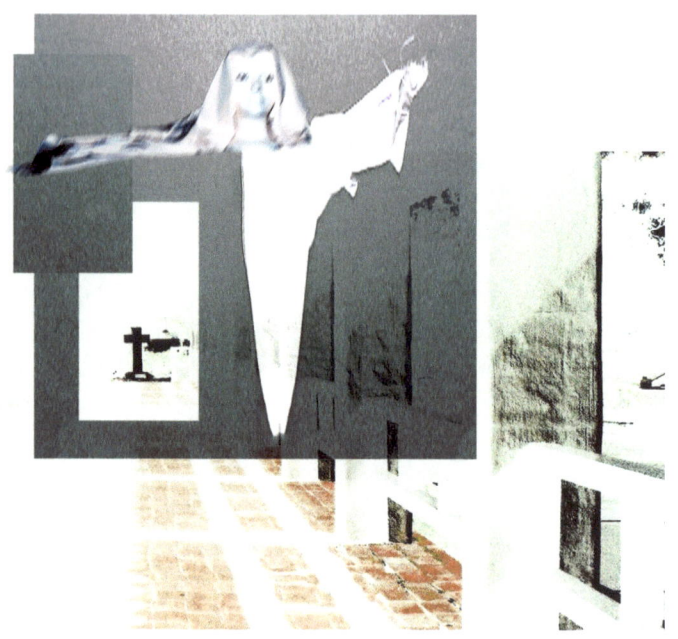

666

add

subtract

multiply

divide

Mathematics

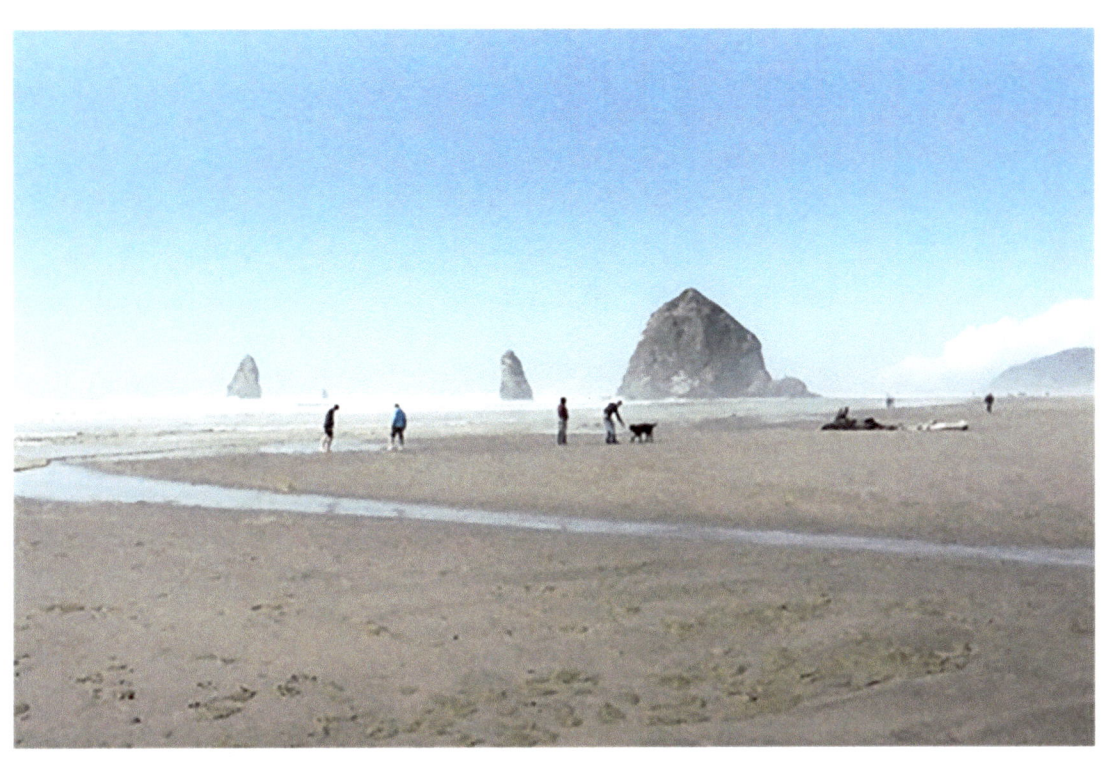

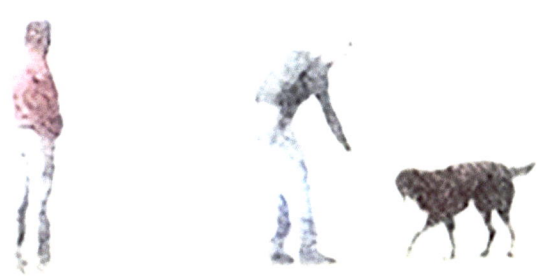

"Have you been here?"

bark bark bark bark bark

"It's Outside."

JON

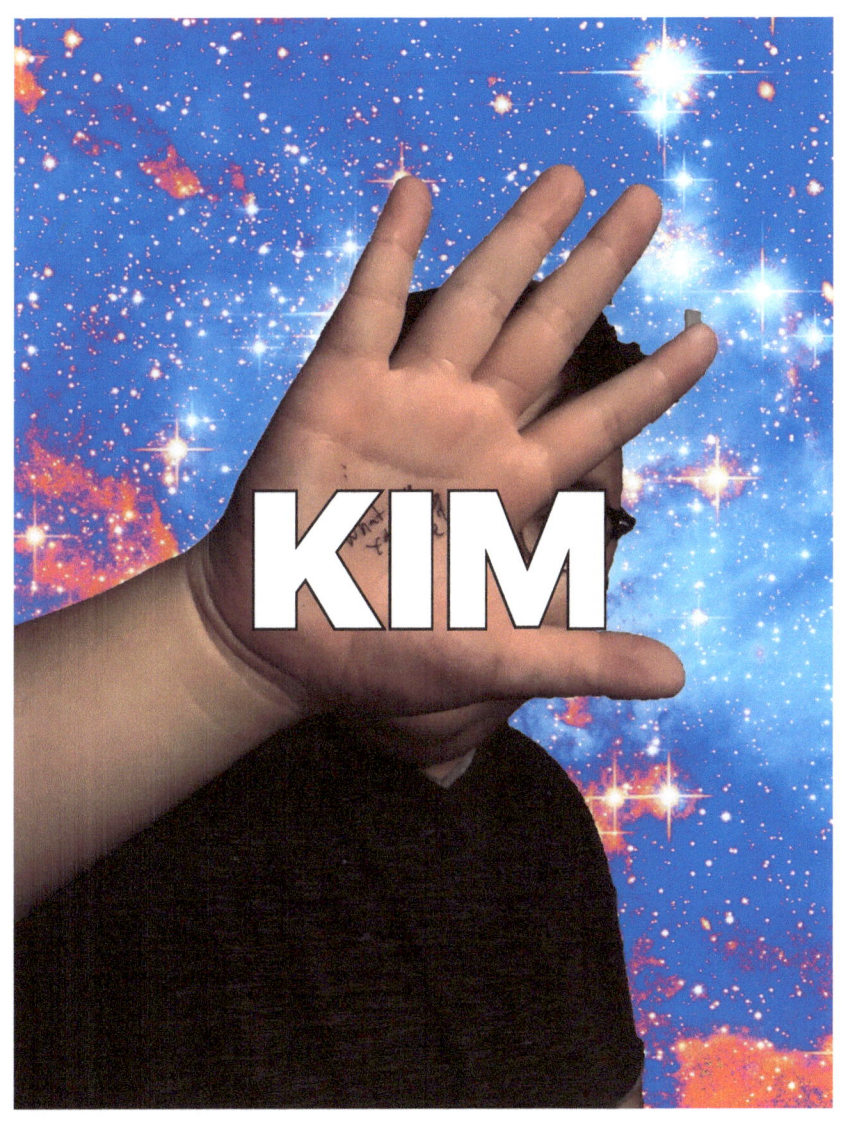

what are you doing dude?

EYE LYE B

SHOT BY ALEC

a cherry grows in my open palm

full price Blistex tie the stem

teeth behind a Volcom hoodie

when i was ten, some white kid

stole my Yugioh cards

blue Hawaii sip and sit on a

beach in Newport smoking a piece of

plastic green and brown glass

trash broke into glittter

bleached roots always wither

blue hair and blonde eyes

EIH TY DO LLA sundress burn't her thighs

shedyed iwannadye (she died) (i wanna die!)

is you a natural brunette? is it fall yet?

the wine stays sour

i wear Jordans in the shower

catching Hermes in the shade

the kids fall off the rye

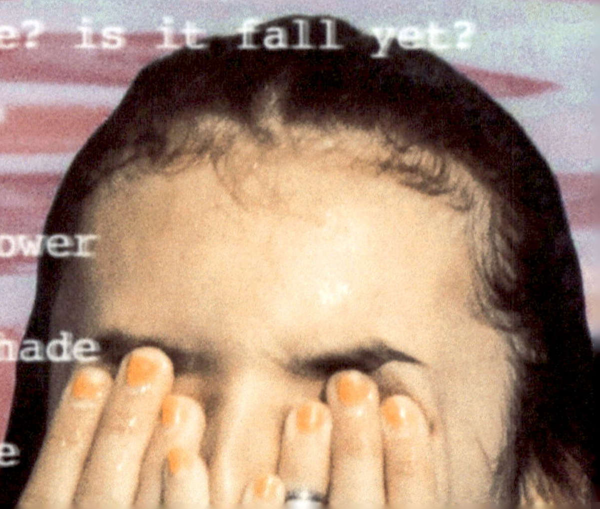

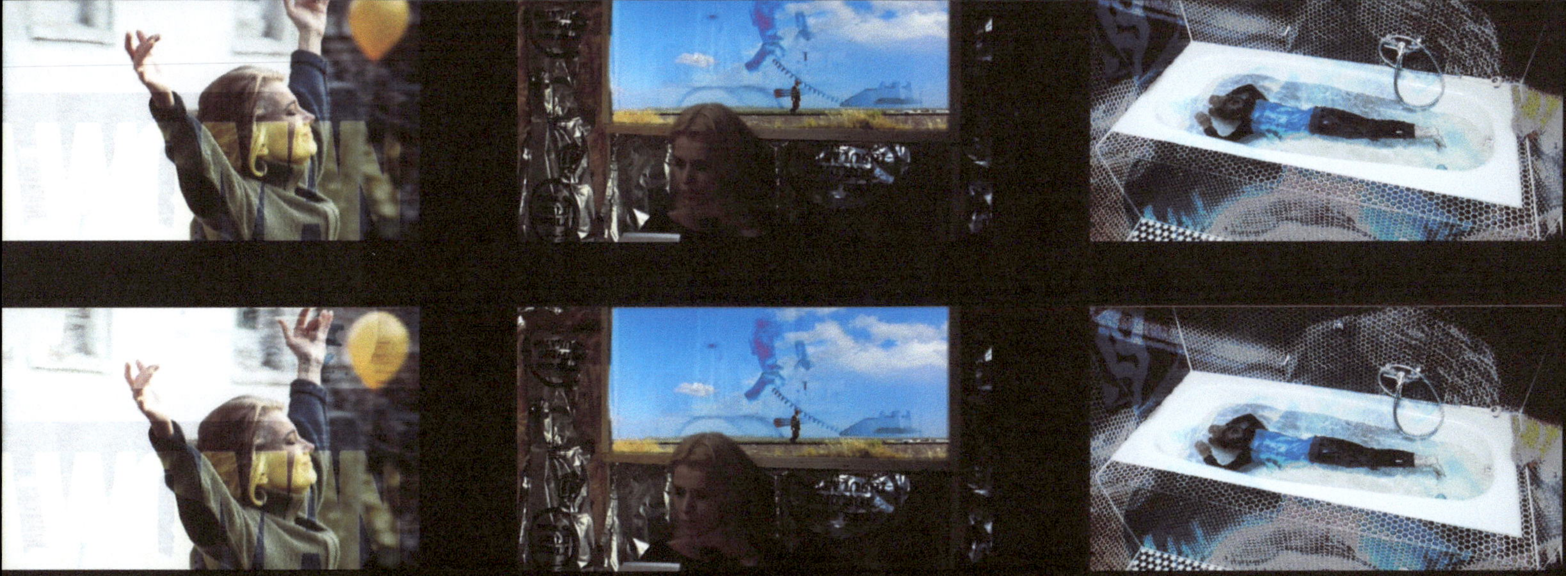

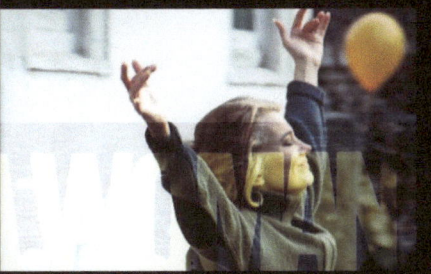
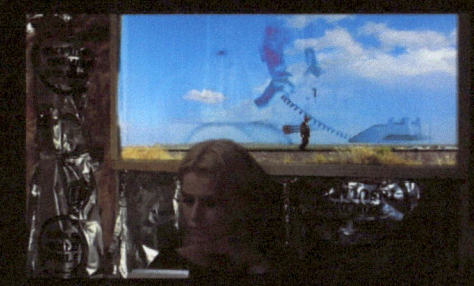
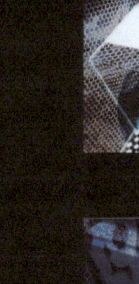
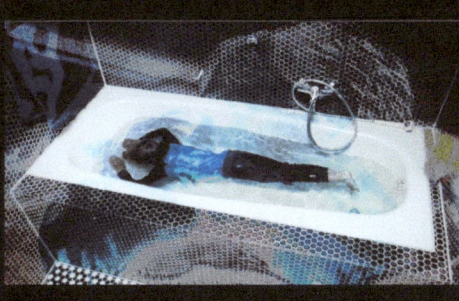

ACROSS
2 why isn't mommy home?
3 monster movie, monster is home (not monster house)

DOWN
1 man is found, gives home

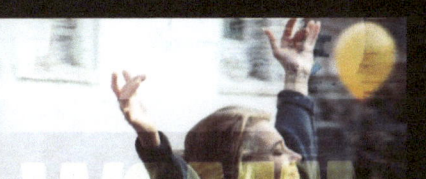
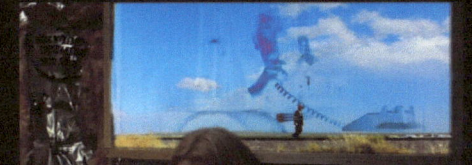
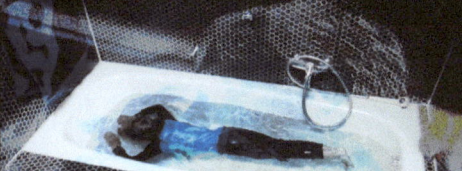

THOMAS

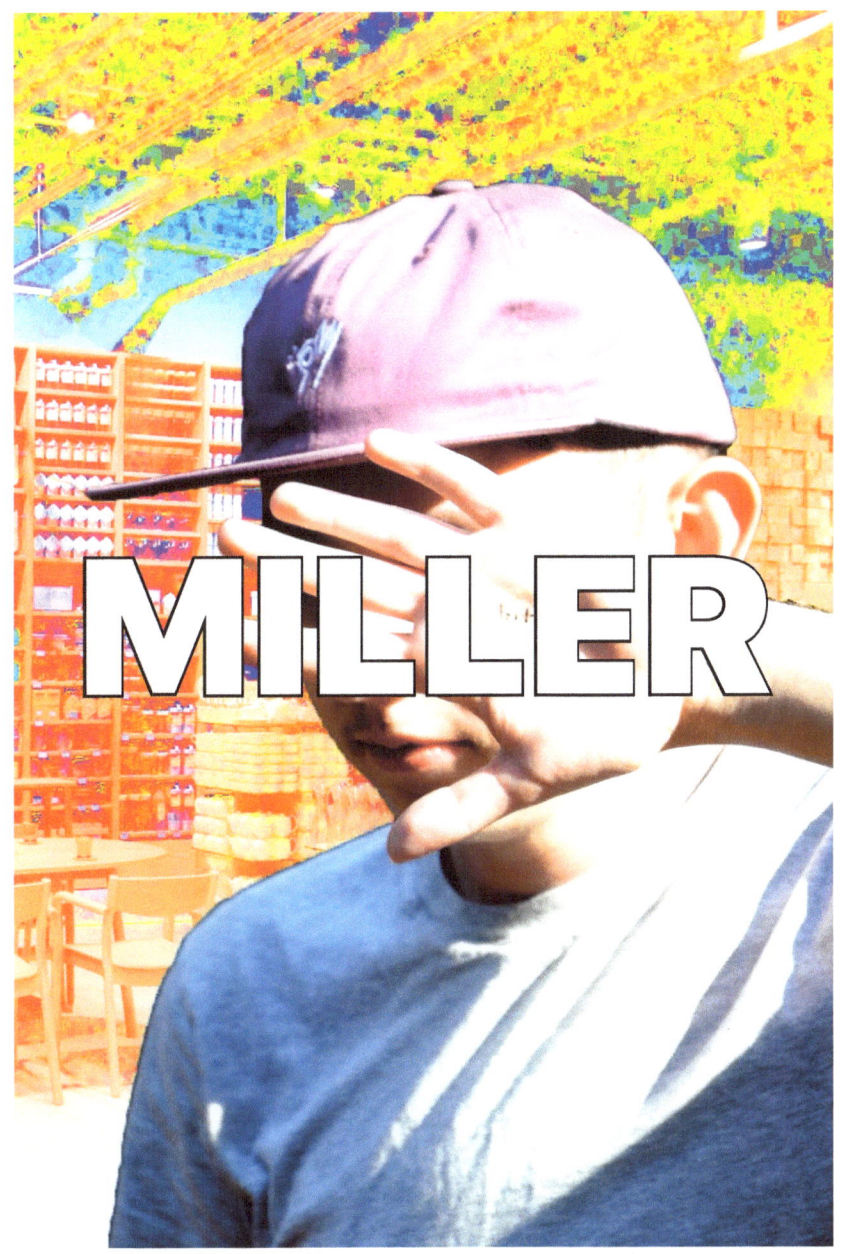

bitch

FALL

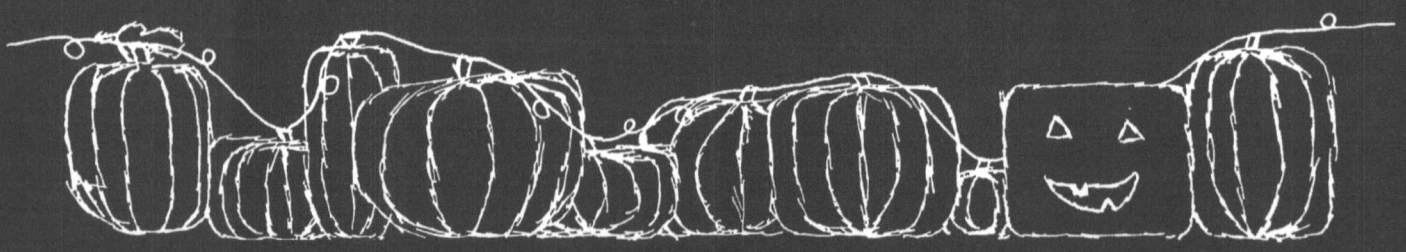

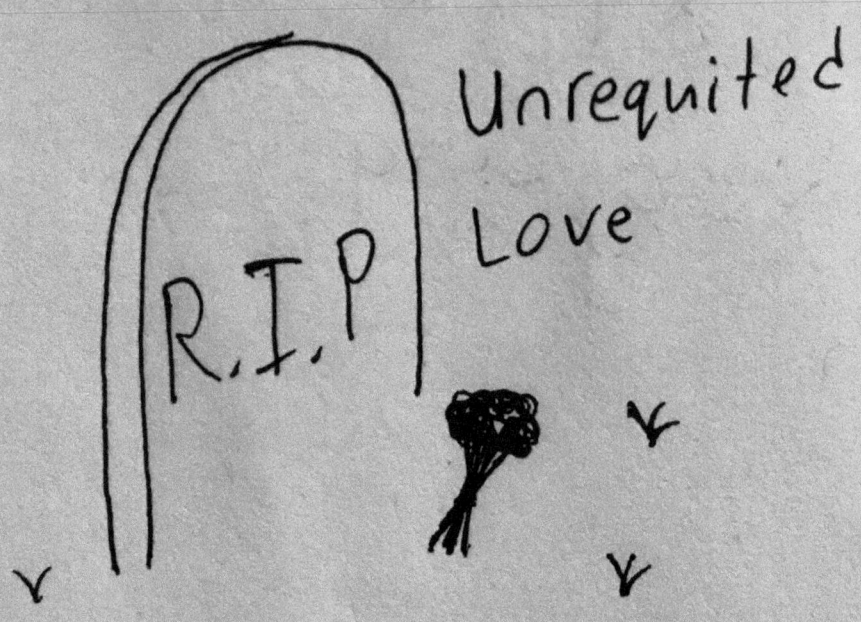
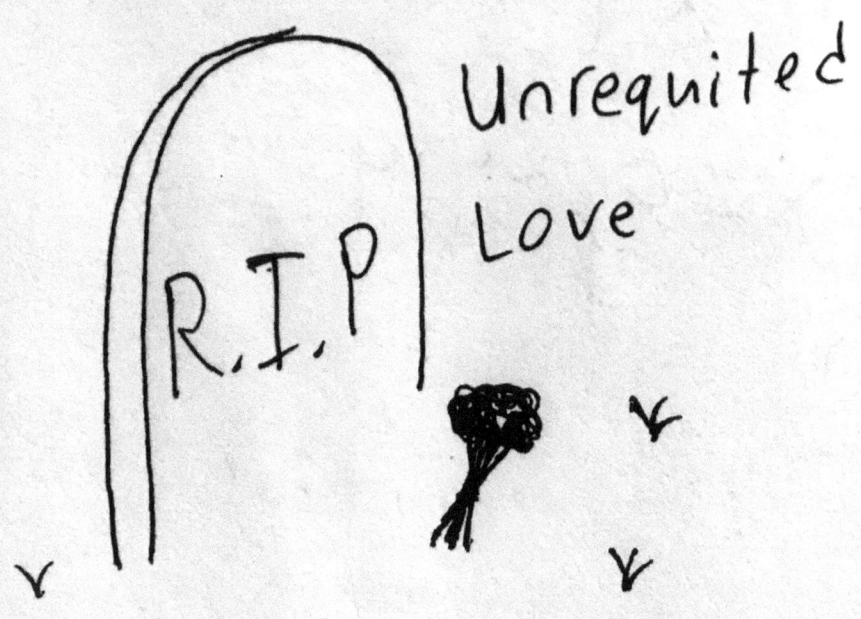

thmlr

thmlr

thmlr

thmlr

thmlr

thmlr

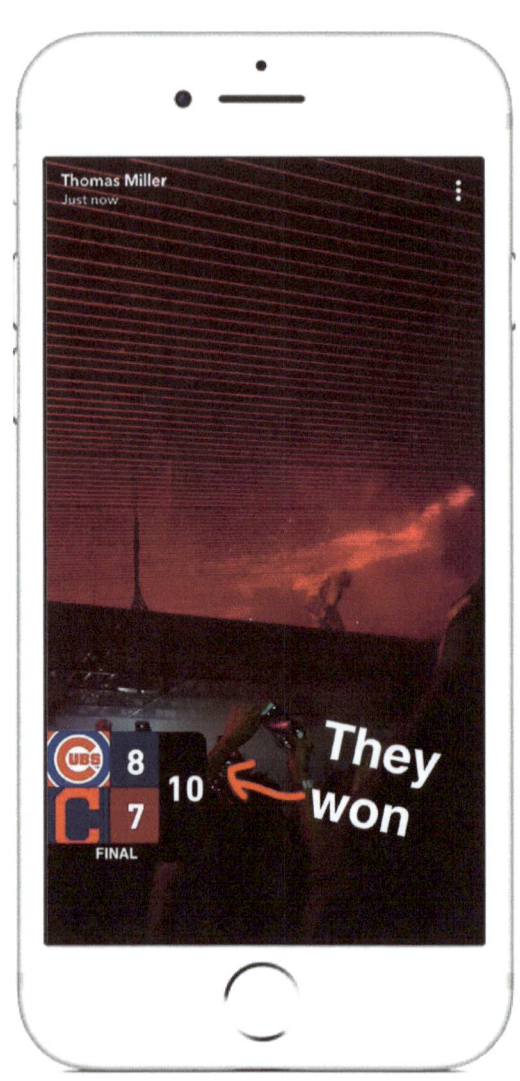

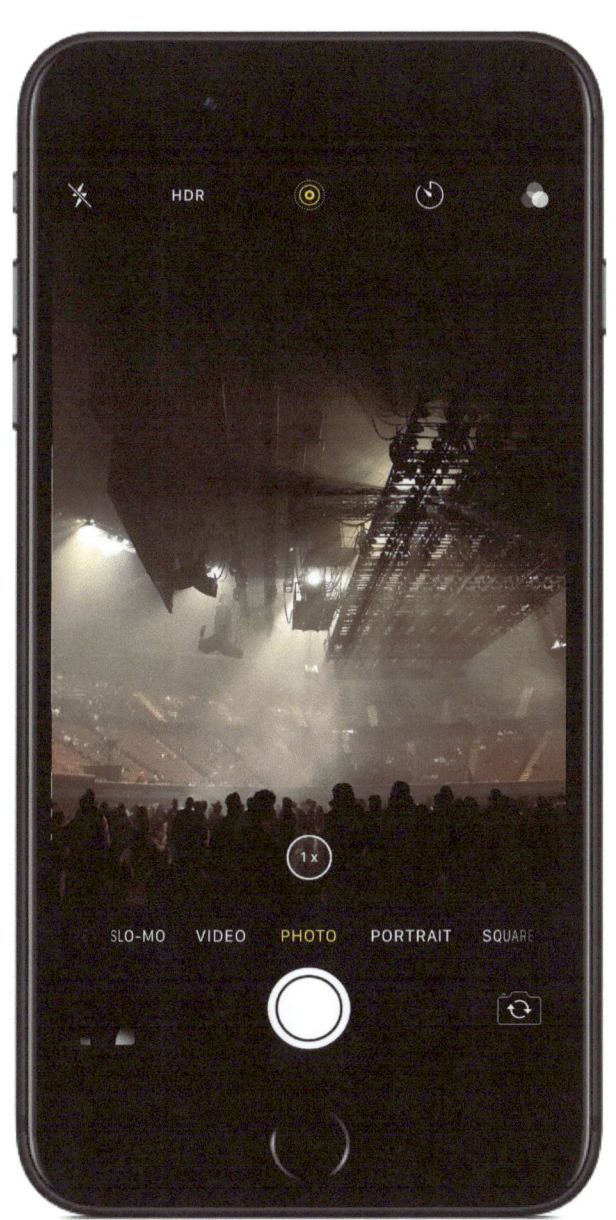

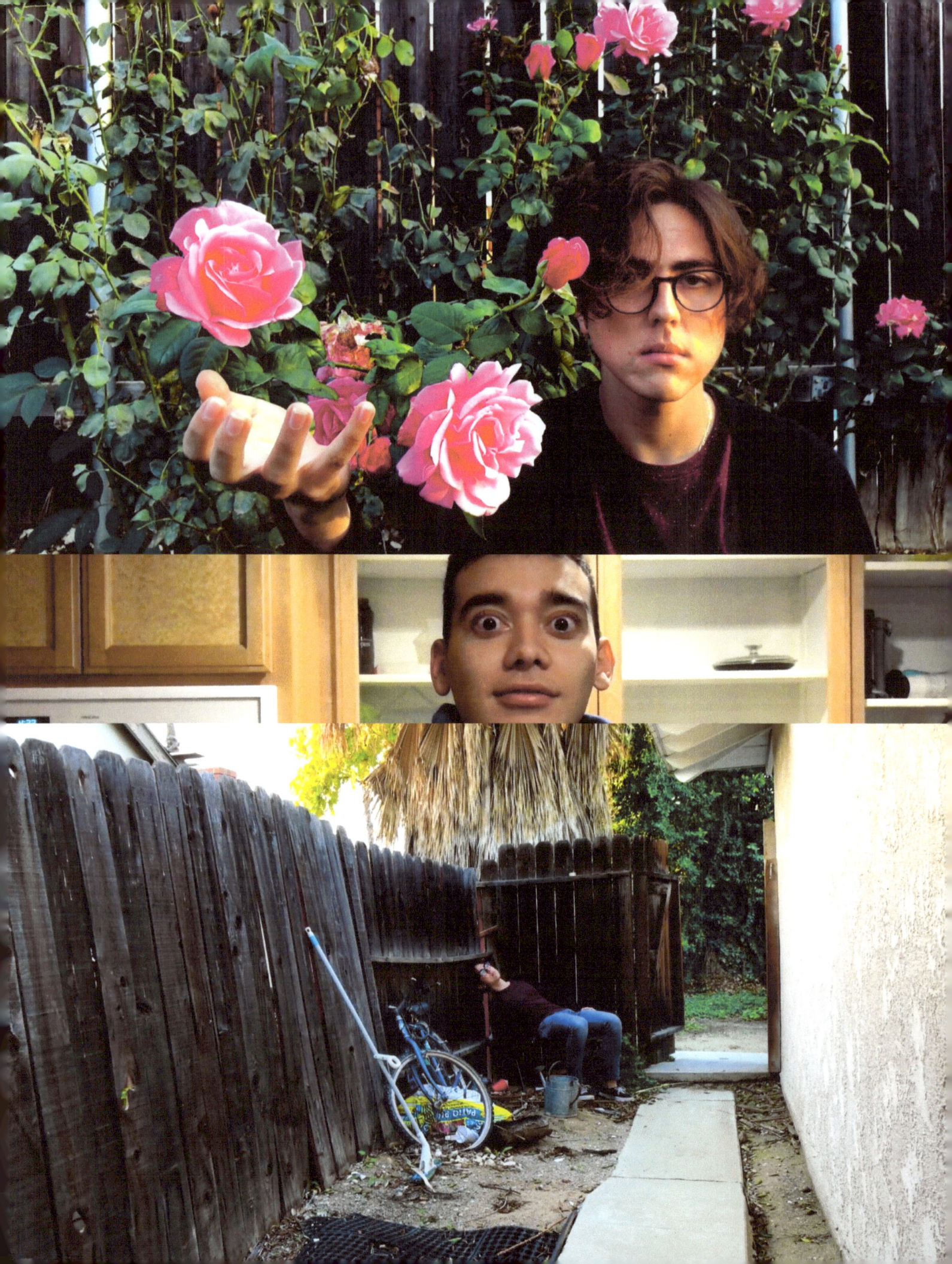

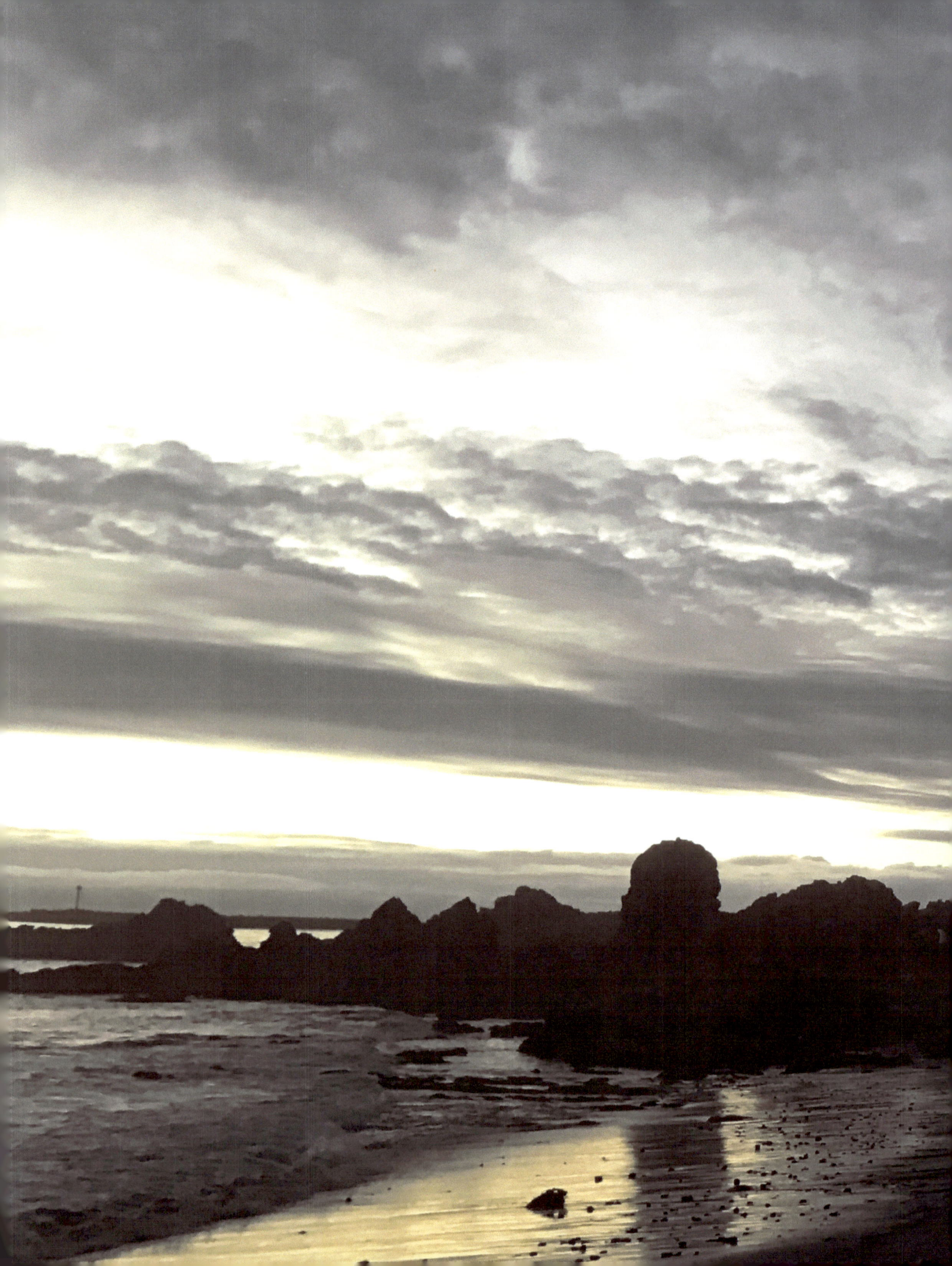

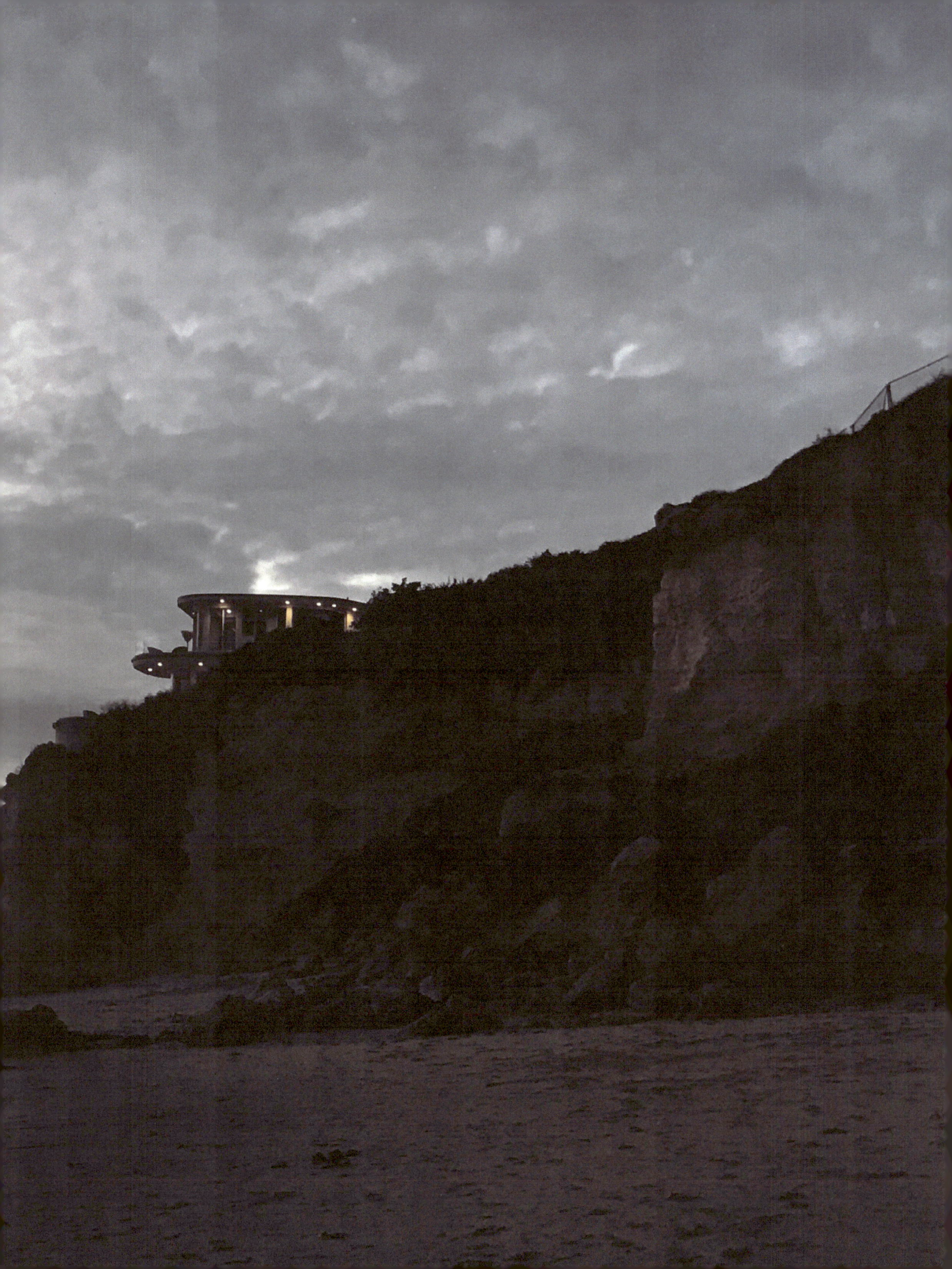

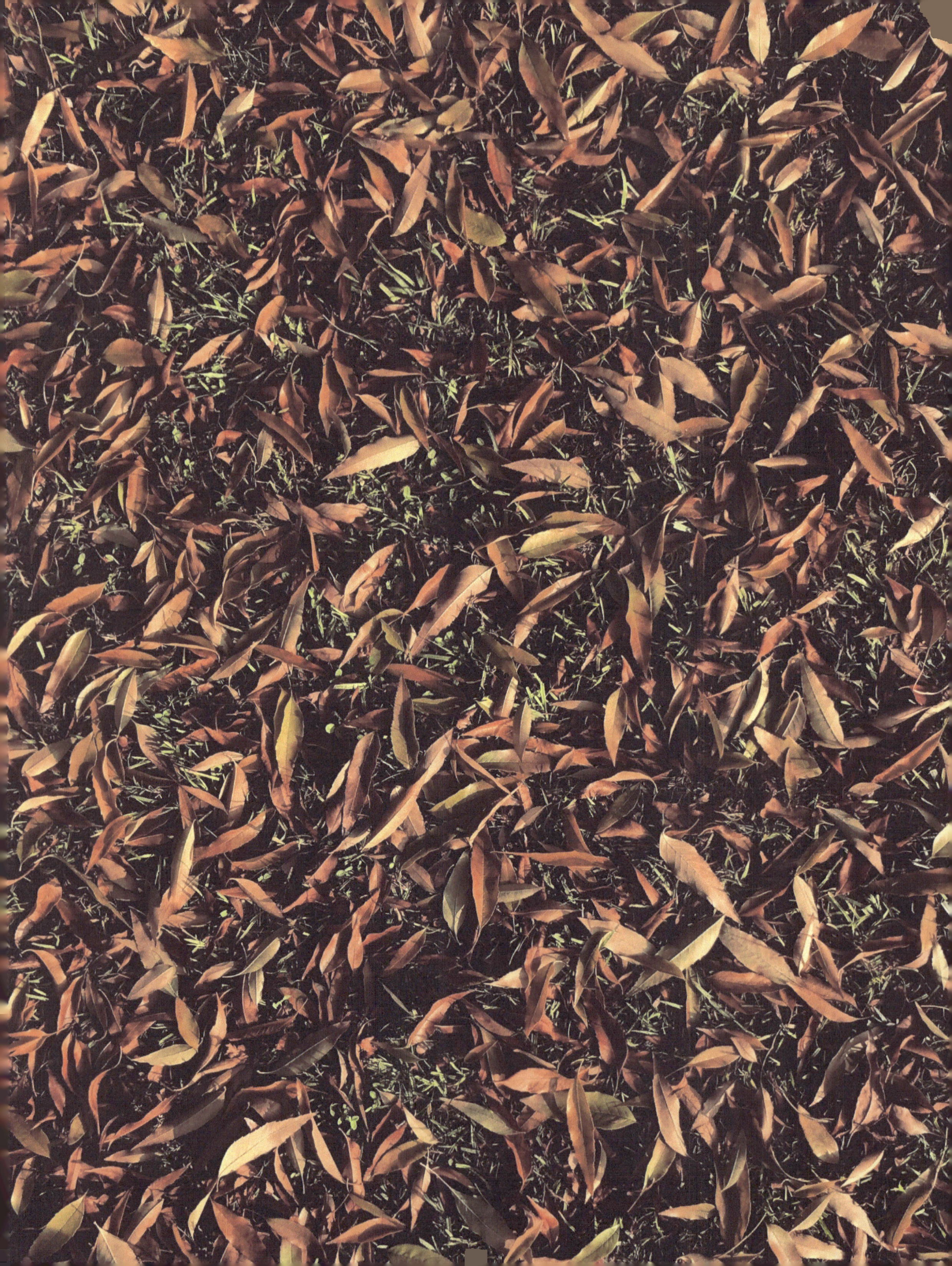

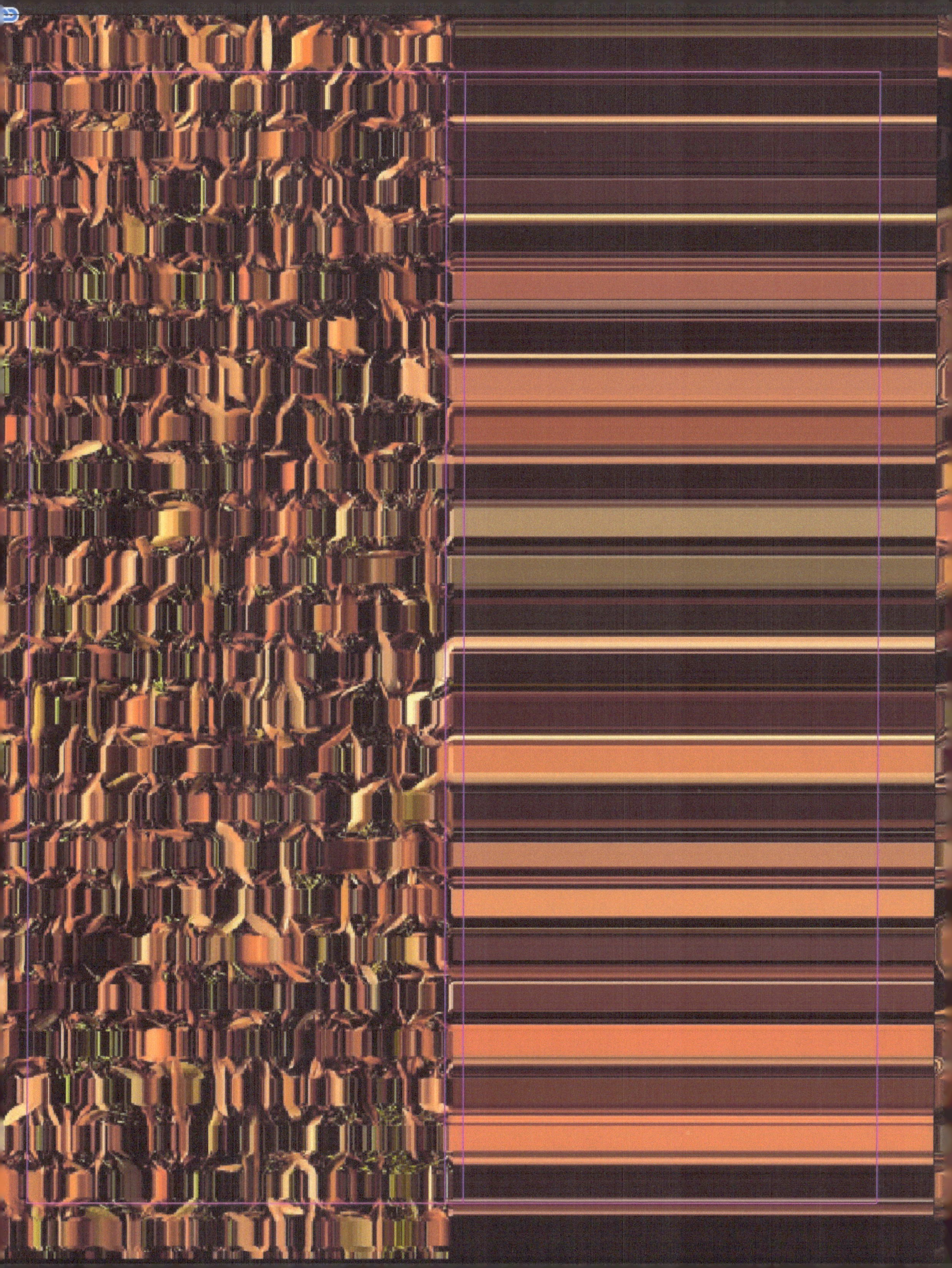

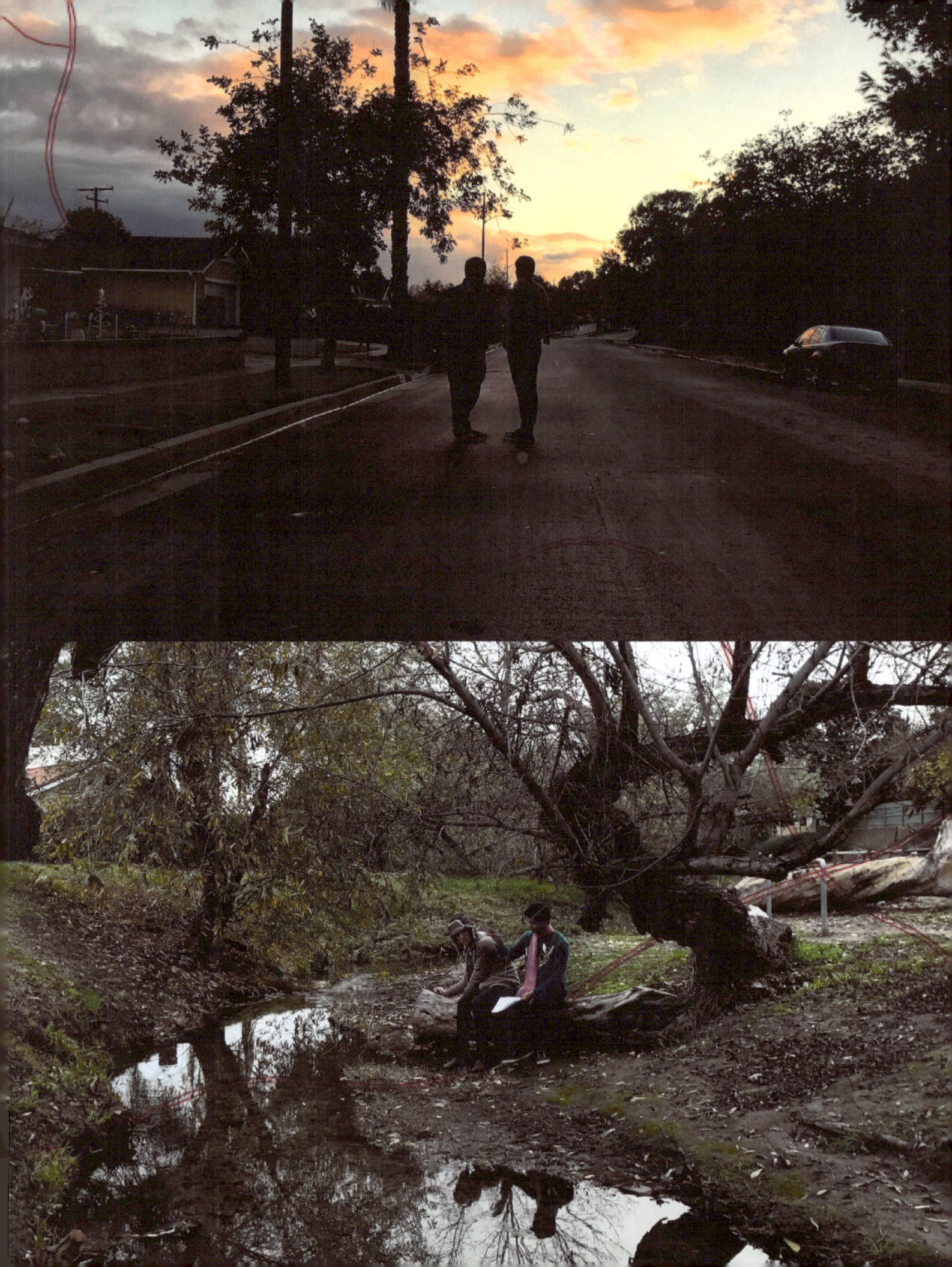

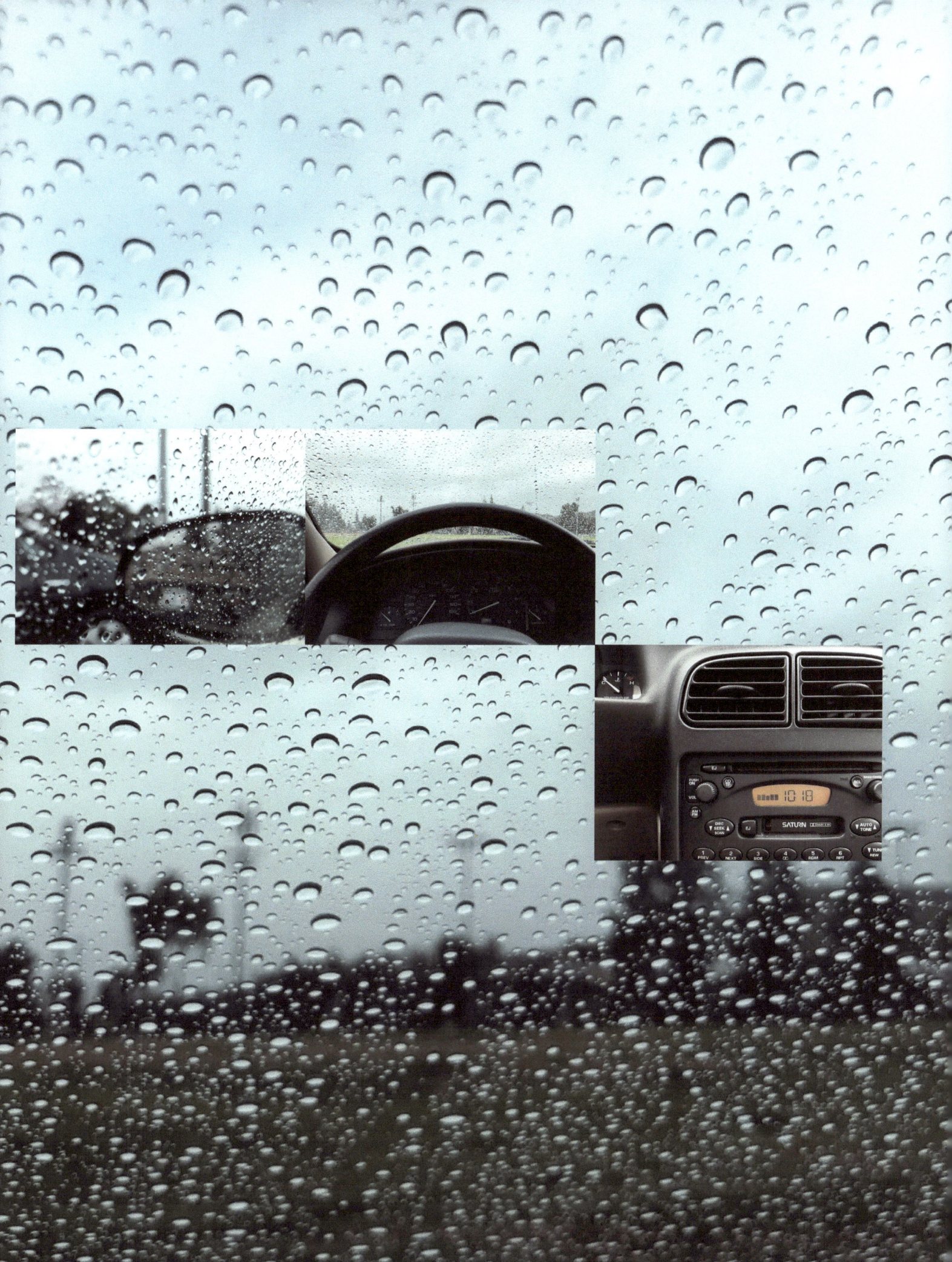

SPRING

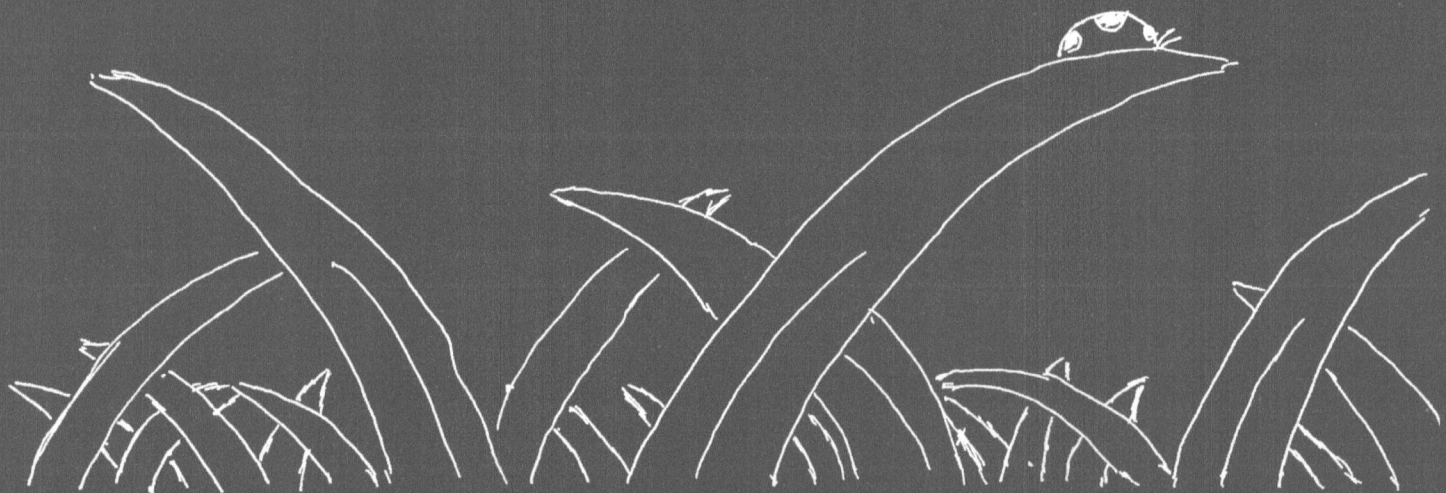

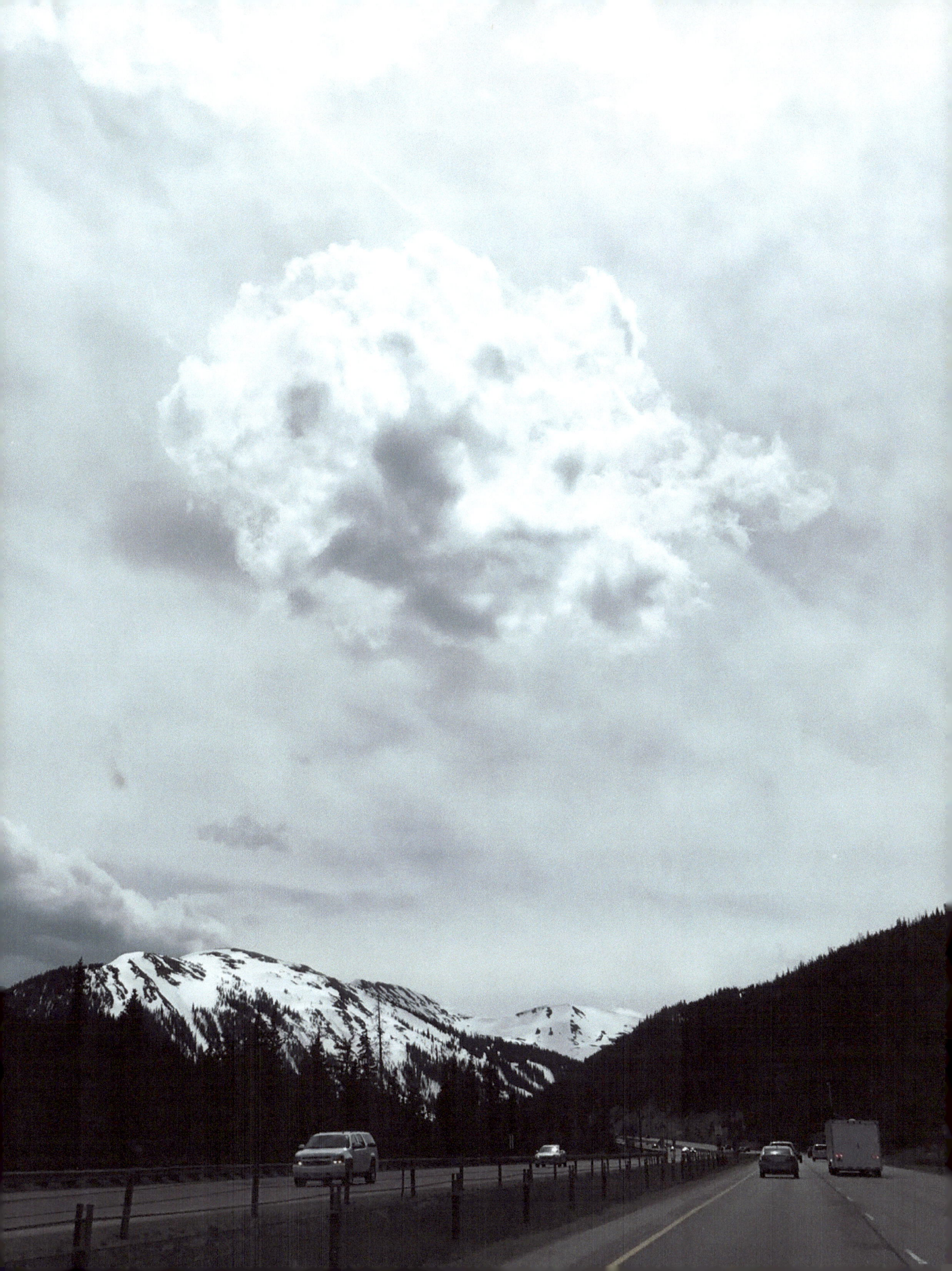

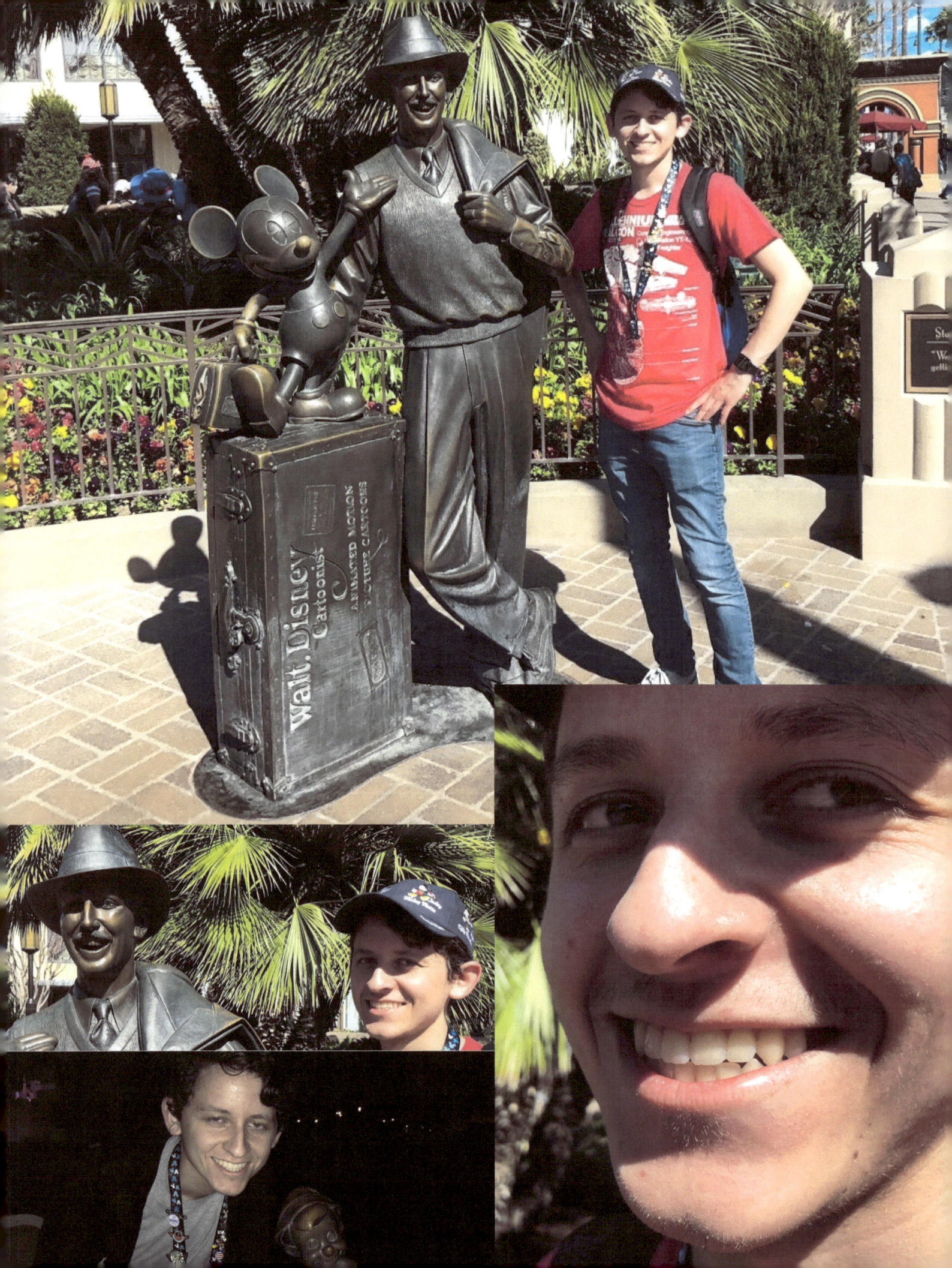

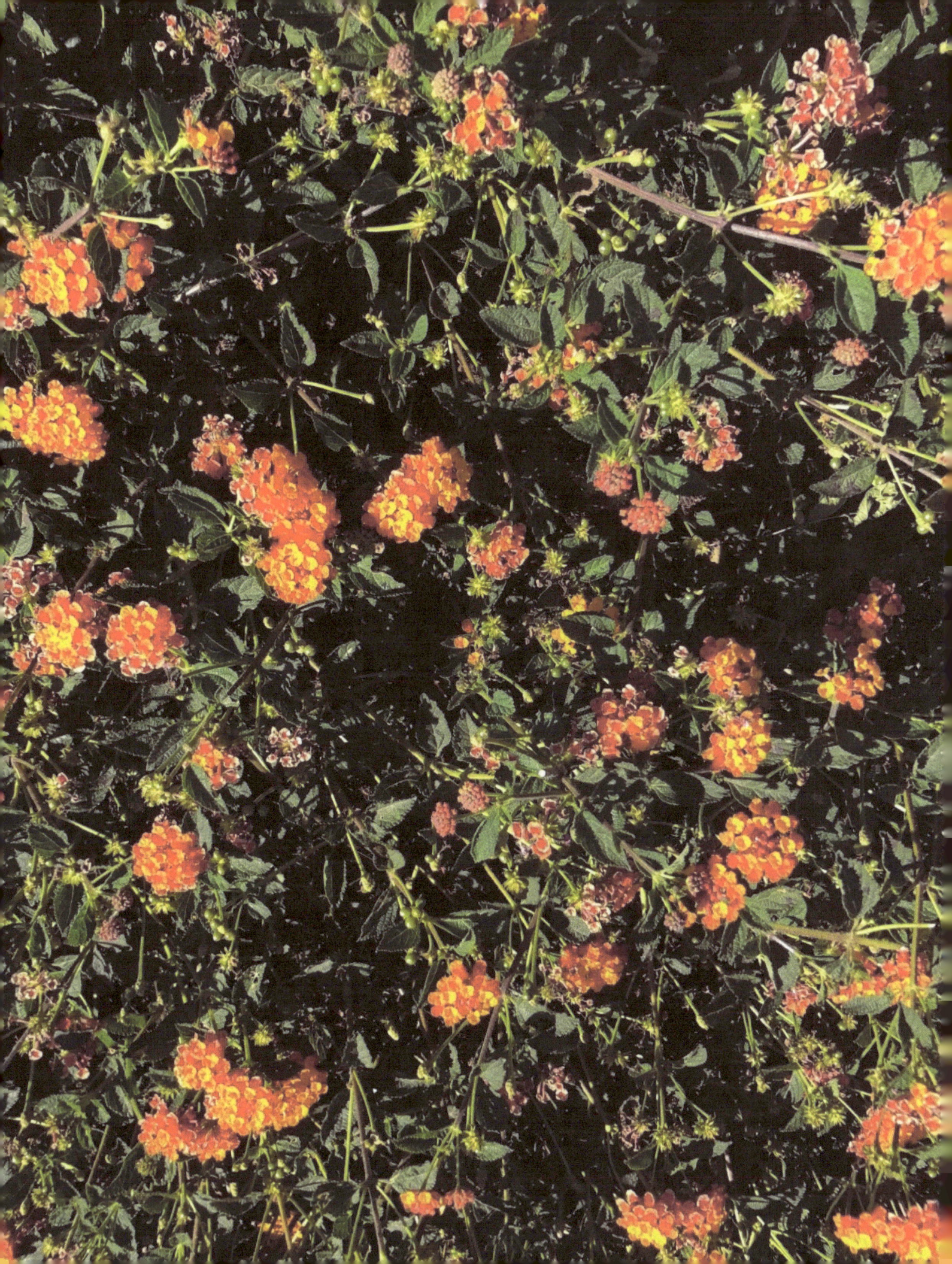

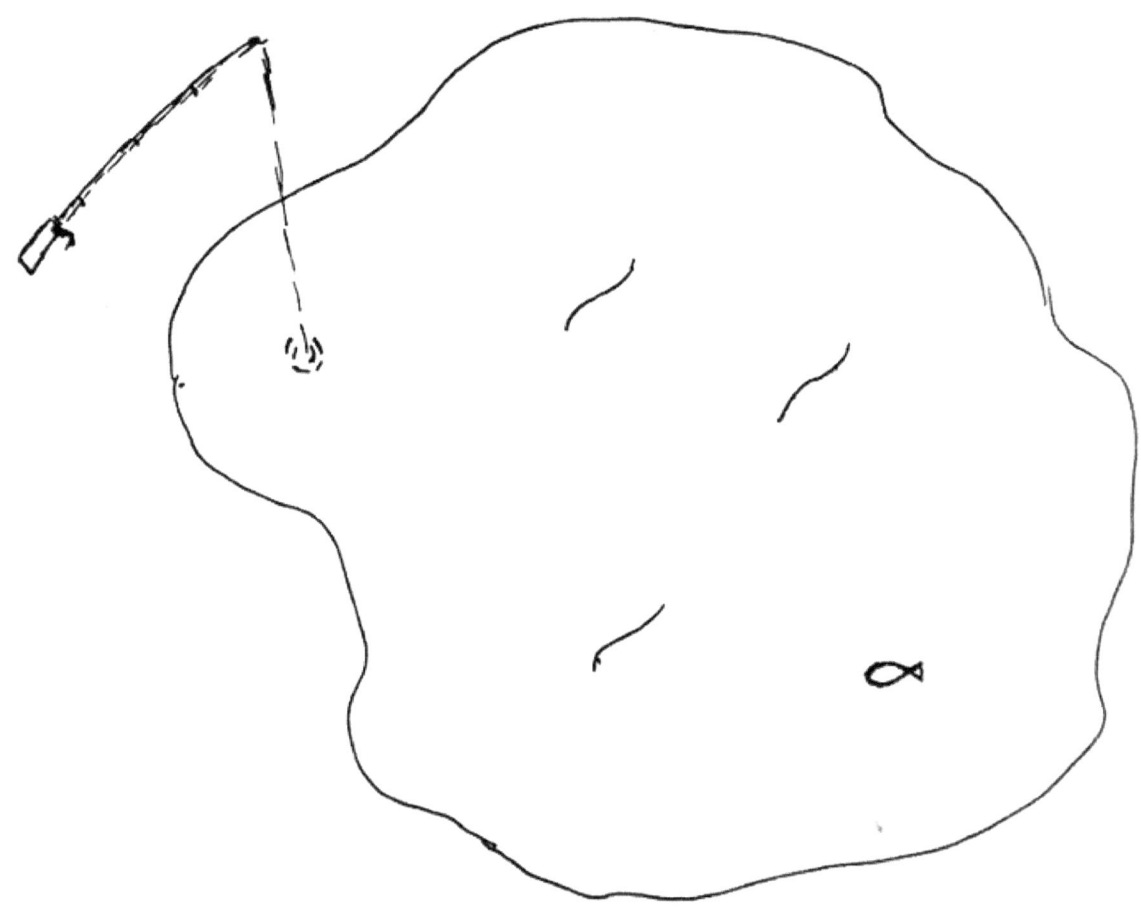

LOSER GANG
"LOSERGANG"

```
L O              L
S E R            U U
G A N G          S E R
                 G A N G
```

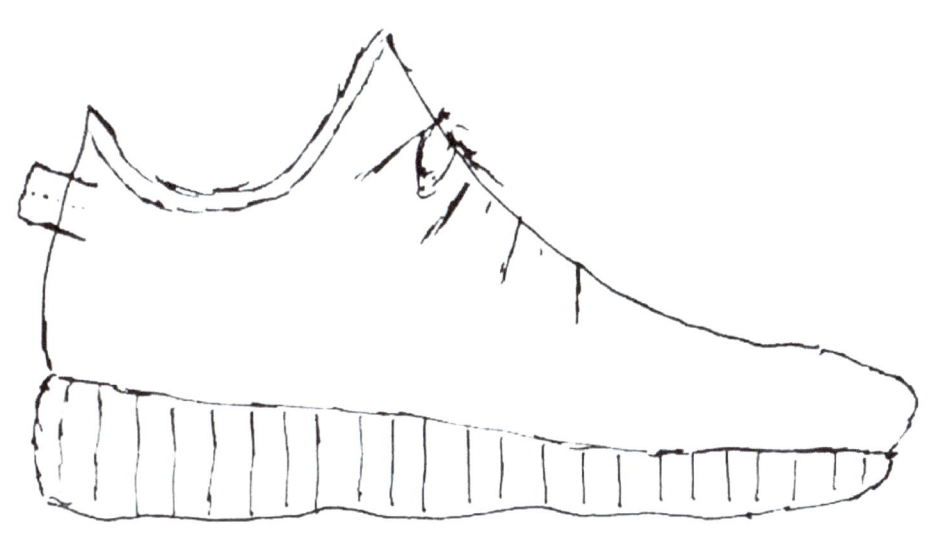

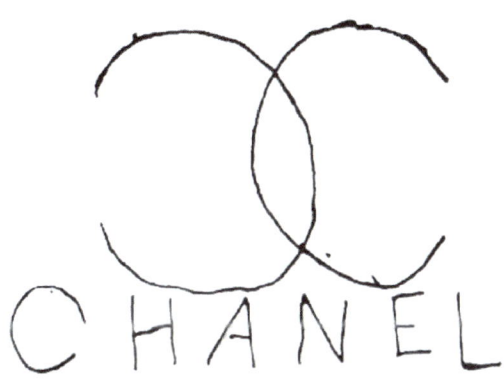
CHANEL

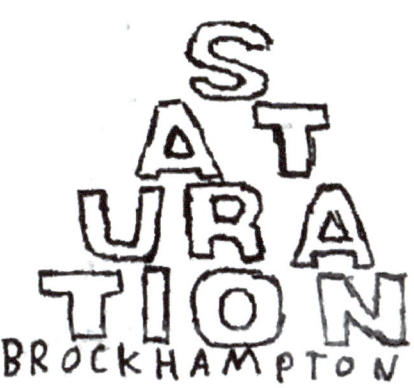
SATURATION
BROCKHAMPTON

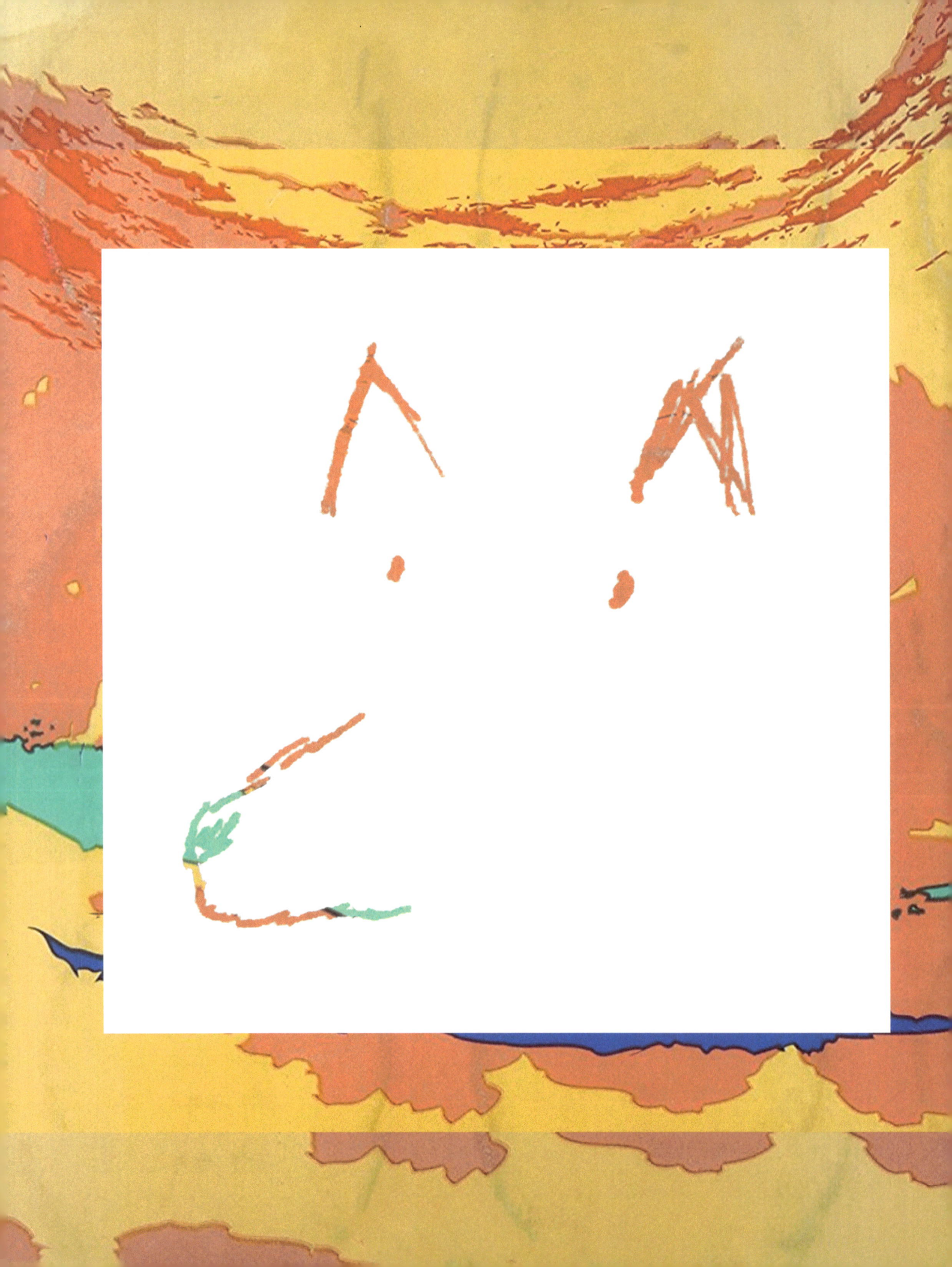

SUMMER

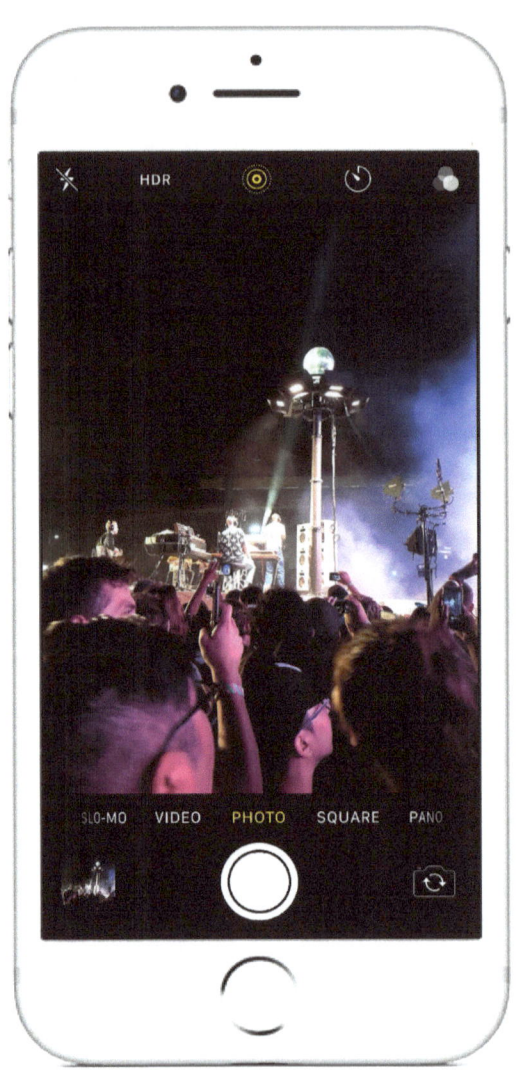

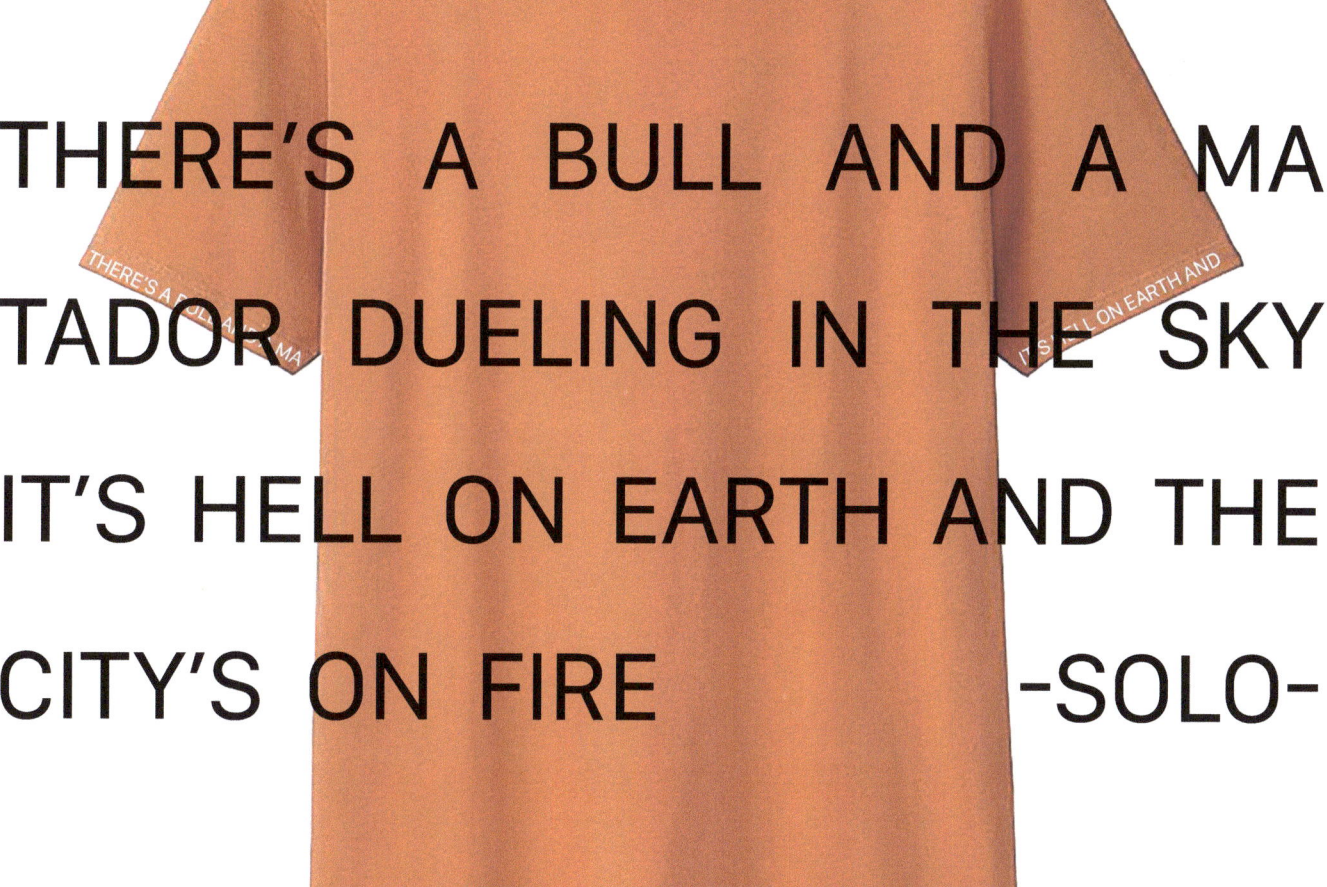

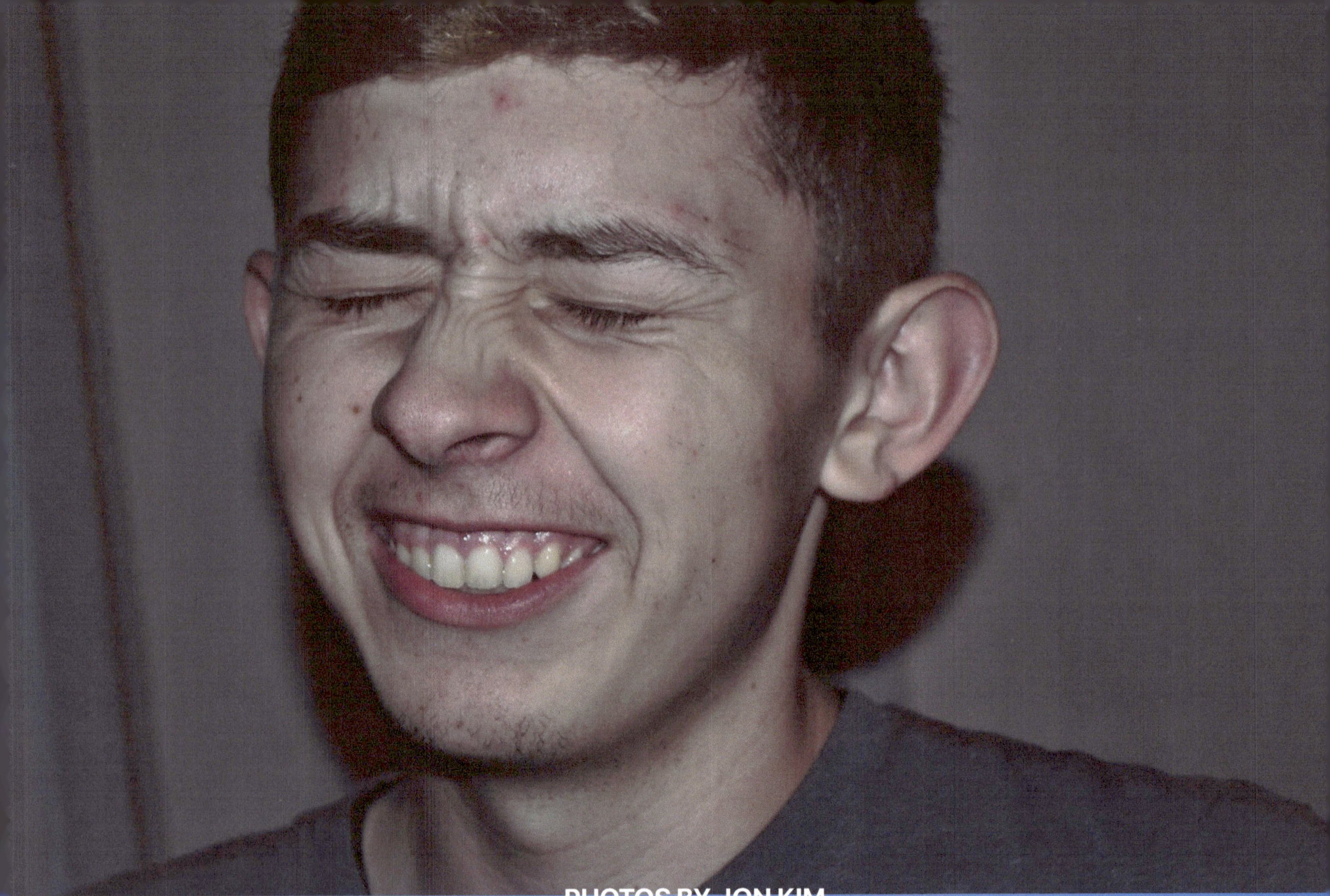

PHOTOS BY JON KIM

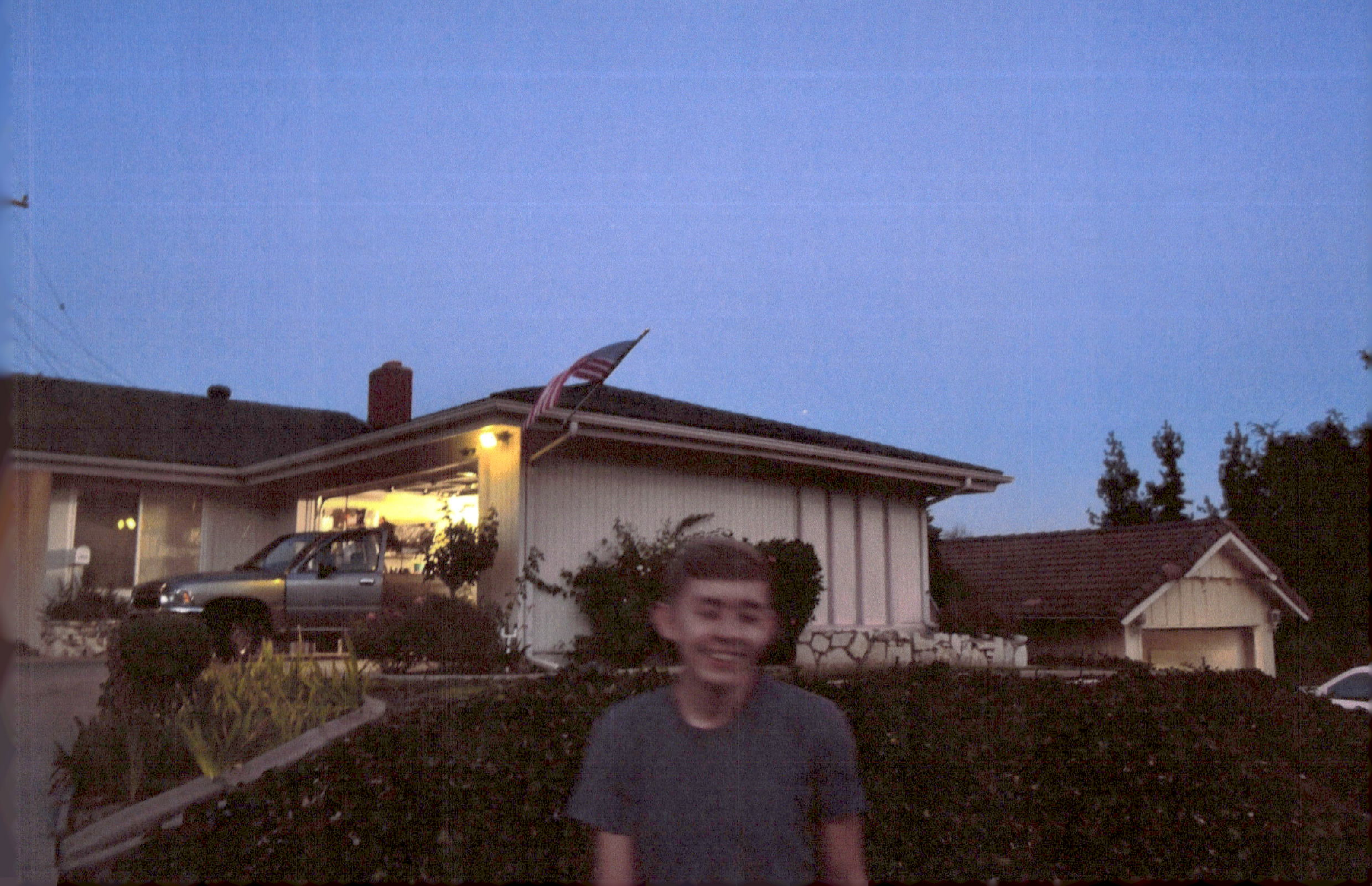

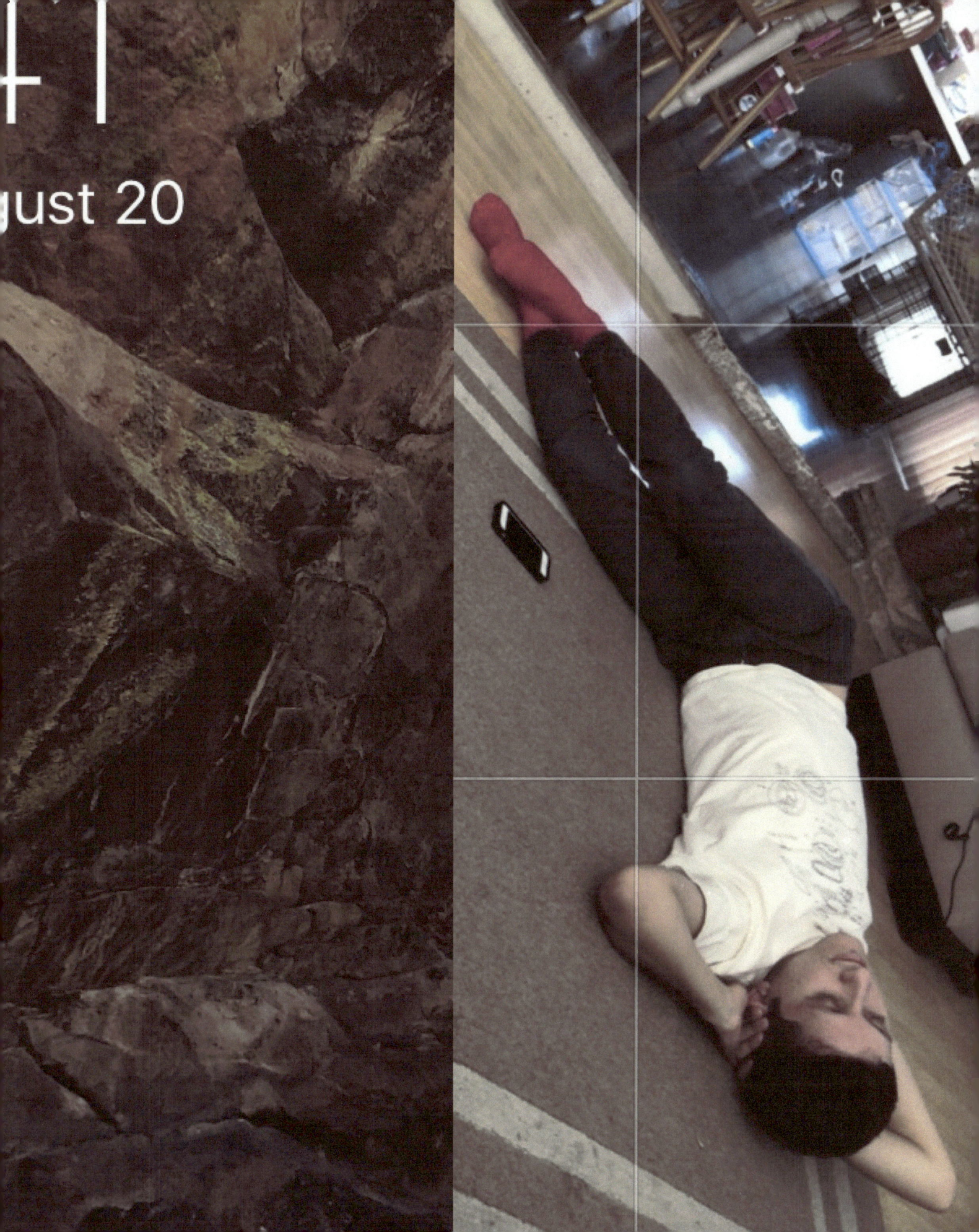

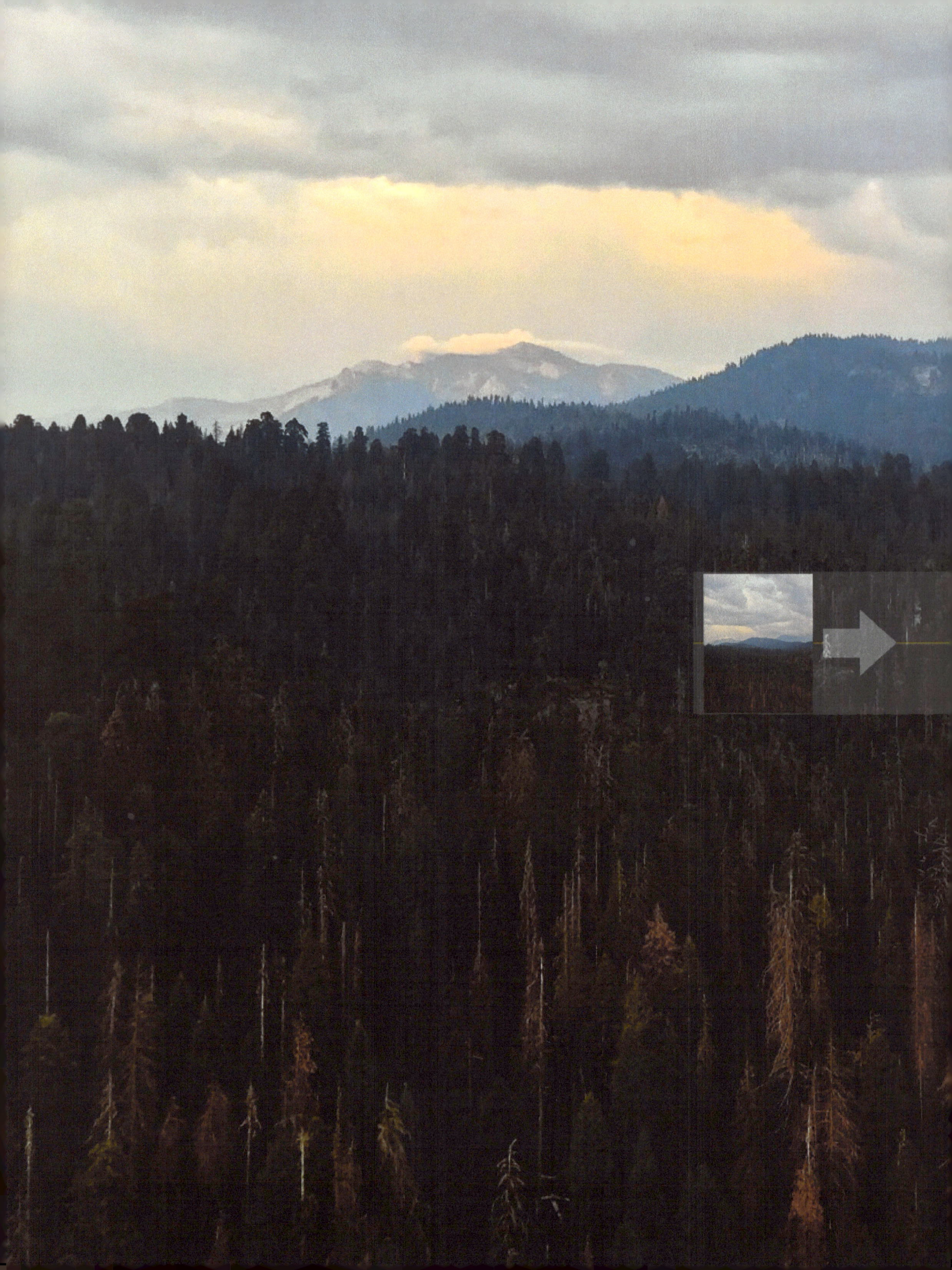

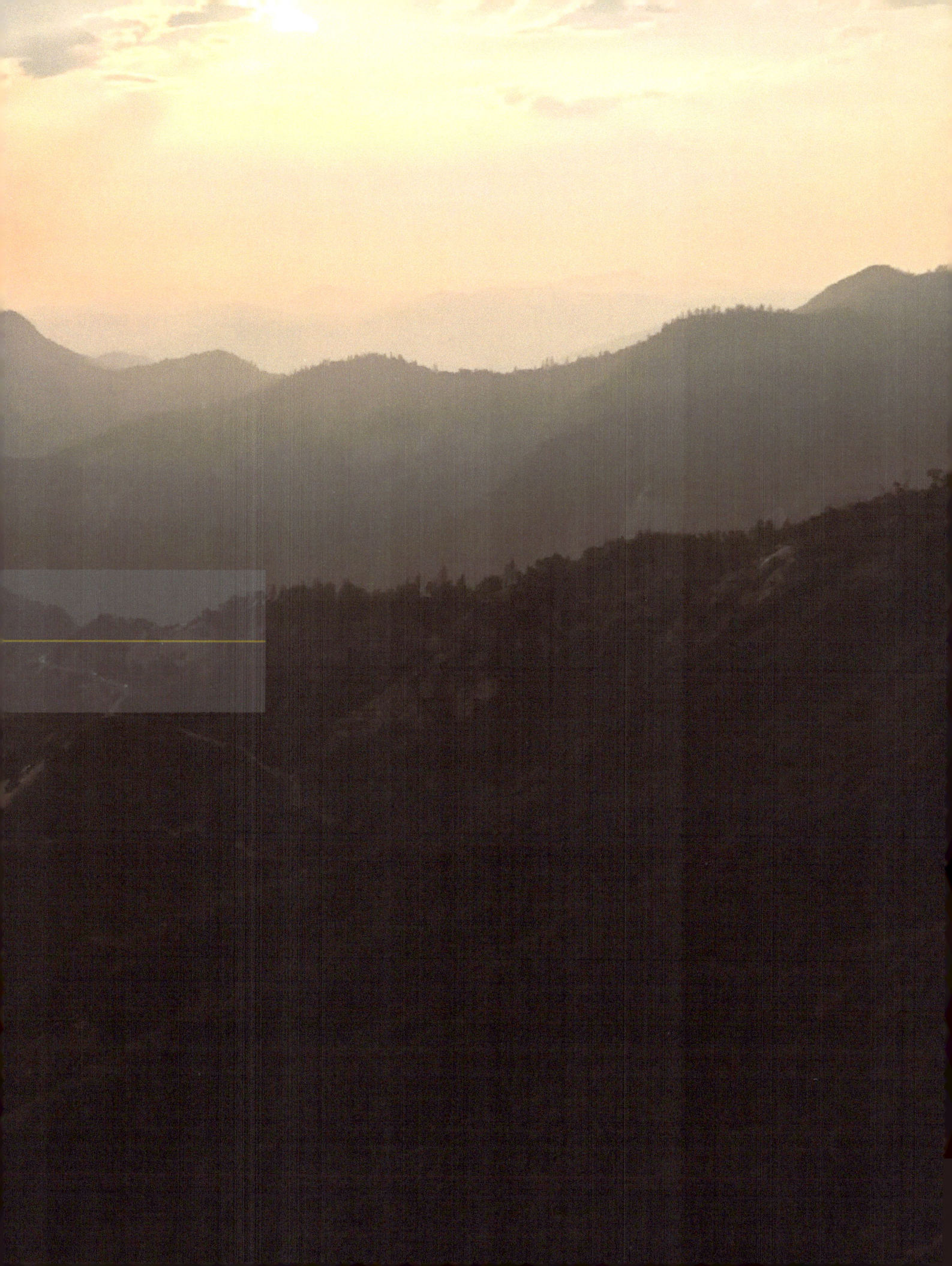

special thanks

JOSE

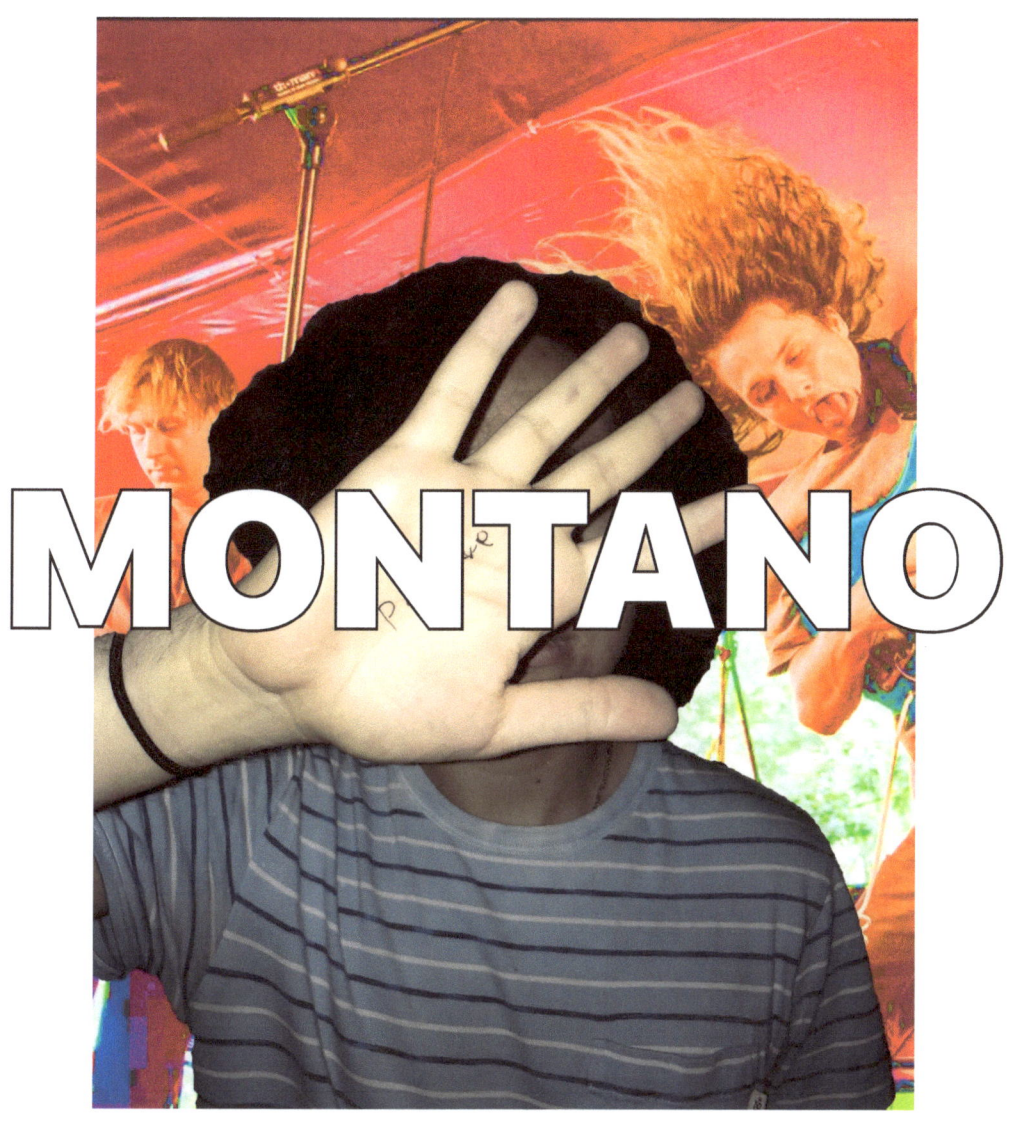

passive

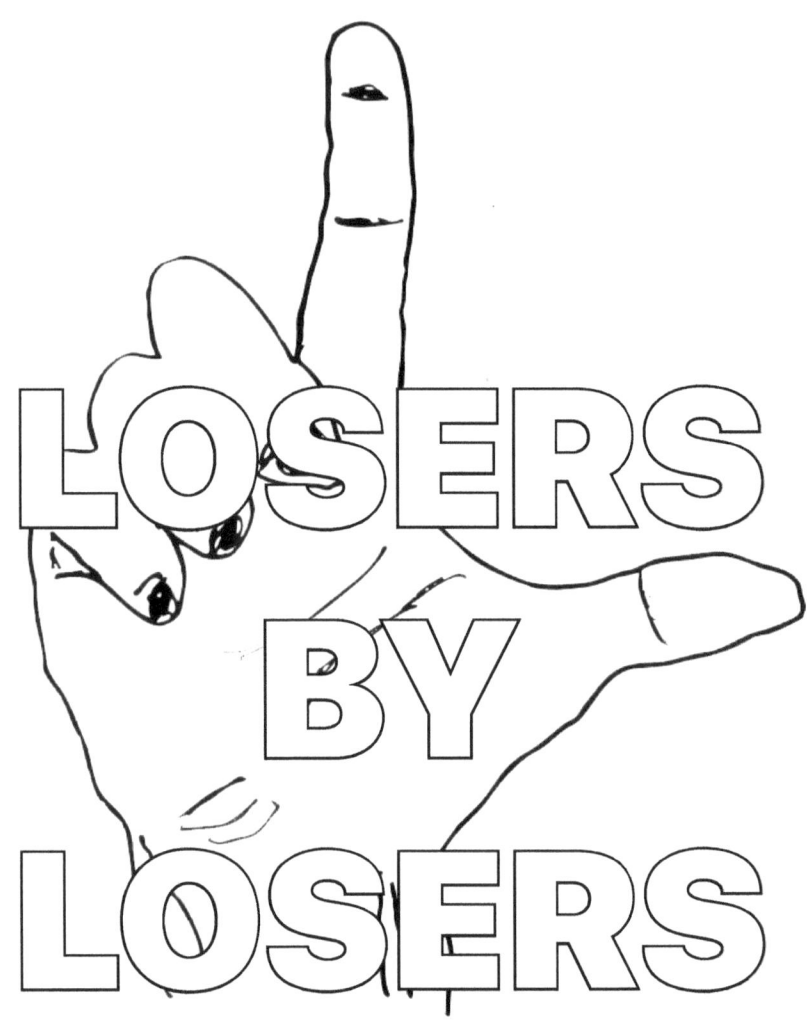

instagram / twitter **losersbylosers**

ALEC LUU

instagram / twitter **aluuser**

soundcloud **boobooluu**

ARON MILLER

instagram **aaaaart.n**

JEAN HSI

instagram **jeanhsi**

JON KIM

instagram / twitter **jonisalright**

THOMAS MILLER

instagram **thmlr_**

twitter **thmlr**

JOSE MONTANO

instagram **j.mntno**

twitter **_hoe_say**

LOSERS MIX 1

www.ingramcontent.com/pod-product-compliance
Lightning Source LLC
Chambersburg PA
CBHW051216220526
45473CB00003B/1049